WOULD YOU HAVE FIRED JUDAS?

*A Call for Christian Soldiers: Rise Up and Claim
Your Rightful Place in God's Army*

"So we keep on praying for you, asking our God to enable you to live a
life worthy of his call. May he give you the power to accomplish all the
good things your faith prompts you to do."
—2 Thessalonians 1:11 NLT

Would You Have Fired Judas? by Thomas Alan Wheeler
Published by
HigherLife Publishing & Marketing, Inc.
100 Alexandria Boulevard, Suite 9
Oviedo, Florida 32765
www.ahigherlife.com

Scripture quotations, unless otherwise noted, are from the New International Version of the Bible. Used by permission.

Paperback ISBN: 978-1-939183-84-2

Cover Design: Dimitreus Castro

First Edition
15 16 17 18 19 20 — 9 8 7 6 5 4 3 2 1
Printed in the United States of America

WOULD YOU
HAVE FIRED
JUDAS?

*A Call for Christian Soldiers: Rise Up and Claim
Your Rightful Place in God's Army*

THOMAS ALAN WHEELER

HIGHERLIFE
PUBLISHING & MARKETING
www.ahigherlife.com

Table of Contents

PART THREE

PART FOUR

PREFACE

"It's so much easier to suggest solutions when you don't know too much about the problem."
—Malcolm Forbes

A skydiver jumps out of a plane at 12,500 feet to ensure a safe landing on the ground below; I feel like I jumped out (fell, was pushed) at 100 feet and my parachute just barely opened before I hit the ground. Effectively helping the homeless in America is much more difficult than I imagined when I moved into urban America. It was like entering a Third World country and wrongly assuming I understood the language because it sounded so much like English. I thought I could help them far more than I was able to do—even now. Poverty is so complicated that it is no wonder many of our middle-class efforts to help the poor fall short. It's also no wonder that people give up. Calling this ministry "hard" is an understatement. Besides the need for training to understand the issues, we need to be in top-notch spiritual shape to endure the schemes of the evil one, and many of us who want to help are not in that condition. I have written this book because this is the book I wish someone had given me before I moved into the Hoskins area in Charlotte, North Carolina.

Fifteen years into this work, I have discovered that helping the poor required a change in my approach to a few fundamental principles in my life, primarily discipleship—the deep, messy, time-consuming discipleship that comes at the cost of numbers. Proper discipleship with those who are hurting the most requires far too much one-on-one commitment for the average person. Therefore, it comes at the cost of what I previously considered success. Dr. Ruby Payne writes in her book, *Bridges out of Poverty: Strategies for Professionals and Communities*, that for a person to move from poverty to middle class or even from the middle class to becoming wealthy, a person must sacrifice relationships.[1] It is similar to the way a newly converted Christian has to sacrifice past relationships upon conversion for the sake of their own maturity. However, my experience suggests that the reverse of her finding is paradoxically true in ministry: in order for a middle class or wealthy person to help the poor, they must sacrifice achievement for relationships. That meant I had to change my definition of success. Mother Teresa said, "God has not called me to be successful. He has called me to be faithful." Success and faith are not always in agreement, at least not the way I thought.

I have also discovered that transforming physical poverty starts with transforming spiritual poverty, and that needs to start with the discipleship of our next-door neighbors and the one who sits next to us in church—not just the person we feel sorry for who is poor. We are called to disciple. We just need to remember its cost when we try to help those in poverty.

The first time I ministered to a local prostitute, I wondered what impact it might have on the level of attacks I would get from the enemy. I soon found out. Suddenly, I was sent anonymous e-mails that appeared to be from a friend but which had pornography attached. In a weak moment, I took the bait and was exposed to a level of pornography I never even knew existed. I did not seek it; it sought me. Was I over my head spiritually? I sought help and struggled to get over it, but it made me wonder: if this was happening to me, could it be happening to others? Of course it was. It was happening everywhere. We just don't hear about it until it's in the news—until something happens that catapults that hidden darkness into the public eye. How many leaders have fallen in the last twenty years because of sexual immorality alone? If this kind of thing is happening to enough leaders in our spiritual institutions, couldn't the end result be rioting in our cities camouflaged by racial tensions? We just don't connect the dots until it is too late. I know that is a giant leap of sorts, thinking the rioting about the amount of force the police use in urban America is really a spiritual battle, but what if it is? It's the

1. Payne, Ruby K., and Philip E. DeVol. *Bridges out of Poverty: Strategies for Professionals and Communities.* Revised ed.

same with leaders. Were they purposely targeted as I was? Our choices have consequences. And those consequences sometimes take a while to appear. Here's an example of the time it takes to connect dots:

In 1971, the Nixon Administration faced re-election. The unpopularity of the Vietnam War was a threat to Nixon's re-election, but so was the soaring price of food. Nixon appointed Earl Butz as Secretary of Agriculture. Butz, who became known as "King Corn," urged farmers to produce massive amounts of commodity crops, particularly corn, in an effort to drive down prices. High fructose corn syrup (HFCS) was produced from surplus corn. HFCS is a very sweet, gloppy syrup that has now been pumped into just about every food we can imagine, making everything cheaper, sweeter, and extending the shelf life of products from days to years.[2] The point? It worked. Since that time, we have been producing less-expensive food. For years, HFCS drove down food prices because of its ability to preserve the life of food. No one knew of anything but its benefits.

But today, although still controversial (similar to our initial understanding of the risks of smoking), some health pundits believe cancer, diabetes, obesity, and heart disease are consequences of this new discovery, particularly since it is the number one source of calories in our diet.[3] Similar to a government supporting a dictator today and then invading that dictator's country tomorrow, HFCS appeared to be a good idea in the beginning, but time may prove it to be the single most important factor, outside of smoking, for you and me to develop a life-threatening disease.[4] Furthermore, if it doesn't kill us, it might just bankrupt us because of the soaring cost of health care. The best solutions are usually more difficult and more costly in the short term; but over the long haul reap a much more lucrative harvest. We just have to have the patience, wisdom, and perseverance to follow them when most people don't or won't. Kathy Rivera, Executive Director of Joseph's Home, a ministry near Charlotte serving disabled kids, once told me, "Tom, everything catches up to us, eventually. It is just a matter of time." She's right. And that is my point about our discipleship process. It might just be catching up to us—now.

Admittedly, there likely are better books than mine covering the facts about poverty and offering more powerful ways to help the poor on a

2. Tellier, Alexandra. "Blame Nixon for the Obesity Epidemic." Los Angeles Times. June 27, 2012. Accessed September 23, 2015.
3. Hyman, M.D., Mark. "5 Reasons High Fructose Corn Syrup Will Kill You." Dr. Mark Hyman. May 13, 2011. Accessed September 23, 2015.
4. Norman. M.D., Philippa. "High Fructose Corn Syrup: A Sweetener to Avoid." — Healthy Brain. Accessed September 23, 2015.

day-to-day level. But these books don't start with the root problem, which is the discipleship process with the man or woman we see in the mirror and our next-door neighbor. Nor do they explain the need to know our specific calling as part of that process. They do not explore the "industry" that people such as me find ourselves in that might be causing the fragmentation of our Christian army. I do not hear many voices addressing the results caused by the misunderstandings between nonprofit ministries and the local churches. For example, sometimes money is used as leverage by well-intended people to achieve improper results for people who don't look or act like "us." That includes our poor.

If you are a ministry leader wondering how to avoid many of the obstacles of working with the poor or how to do it more effectively, if you are members of a church wondering how to have an even greater impact in your city, if you are starting an urban ministry or thinking about starting one, if you are a church leader who wants to dig deeper into discipleship, or if you are just a Christian who wants an alternative way to minister to your neighbor for the sake of your children's future, this book might be well worth your time. As I said, it is the book I needed to read before I moved in to the "hood," but that I did not find on the shelves of the local bookstore.

> Timely advice is lovely, like golden apples in a silver basket. To one who listens, valid criticism is like a gold earring or other gold jewelry. Trustworthy messengers refresh like snow in summer (Proverbs 25:11-13 NLT).

May God bless you and continue to use you as a soldier in His army, and may He awaken you if you have been sidelined.

Tom Wheeler
Charlotte, NC
November 14, 2015

INTRODUCTION

Drill Sergeant: "Gump! Why did you put that weapon together so quickly, Gump?"

Forrest Gump: "You told me to, Drill Sergeant."[5]

ONE OF THE TWELVE

Judas was a traitor. He sold out Jesus to the authorities for thirty silver coins that ultimately put Jesus on the cross. Understanding the severity of what he had done, he hung himself. That is what we learn from the Bible about one of Jesus' twelve disciples. What is rarely discussed, however, is the fact that Jesus *chose* Judas as one of His twelve *knowing* that Judas would put Him on the cross:

> Then Jesus replied, "Have I not chosen you, the Twelve? Yet one of you is a devil!" (He meant Judas, the son of Simon Iscariot, who, though one of the Twelve, was later to betray him) (John 6:70-71).

Who would do such a ridiculous thing? We wouldn't. Besides the threat on our lives, Judas would have been considered a threat to productivity, or perhaps deemed mentally ill, and therefore not worthy of being on our team. We might make the mistake of hiring him today, since we don't know the future as Jesus did, but we would certainly fire him before he could do too much damage. Wouldn't we? Don't we?

---

5. *Forrest Gump*. Directed by Robert Zemeckis. Performed by Tom Hanks and Afemo Omilami. Paramount Pictures, 2001. Film.

Let's face it: what Jesus did was insane. He should have saved himself by getting rid of Judas. Then He could have helped even more people in His lifetime. But Jesus never focused on a large group of people. His ministry was to twelve men primarily. Every person mattered and every one had the right to their own free-will choice. Jesus allowed Judas the exercise of that choice to betray him, knowing it would cost Him His life. He also knew this would secure the right for many others to come to know Him one-on-one. Jesus continues to allow each of us the exercise of our free-will choices today, and He continues to focus on singular personal relationships. That reminds me of a story from a contemporary movie, *Saving Private Ryan*, and another question. Given the choice, would I save Private Ryan?

SAVING PRIVATE RYAN

The setting of the epic drama *Saving Private Ryan* (1998) is the Allied invasion of Normandy during World War II.[6] The movie is fiction, but it is based on the true story of the Niland brothers from upstate New York. In the movie, the United States and its allies are fighting against the Axis Alliance of Germany, Japan, and Italy, which threaten the freedom of the world. As the US Army Chief of Staff learns that a Mrs. Ryan is going to get a telegraph about the death of three of her boys killed in action, he discovers there is a fourth boy, Private James Ryan, still in the war. Out of sympathy for Mrs. Ryan he sends orders down the ranks for a group of soldiers, led by Captain Miller and his Second Rangers, to bring the fourth son safely home. They are no longer to engage the enemy for the sake of the freedom they signed up to protect. Instead, they are only to fight when necessary to accomplish their new mission: saving Private Ryan for the sake of a grieving mother.

IS HIS LIFE WORTH MINE?

Perhaps you can imagine what it felt like: landing on the beach at Normandy, watching men dying all around you, as you and your squad survive. Now it's your turn to fight back. About that time your commanding officer informs you of another mission: to save some unknown private. I wonder if we would have felt like they did—outraged.

No offense to Mrs. Ryan, but if the war was lost, her fourth son's freedom would also be lost. The cause was greater than her son. They had signed up to protect the freedom of the United States from a foreign enemy, not try to save

---

6. *Saving Private Ryan*. Directed by Steven Spielberg. Performed by Tom Hanks. DreamWorks Home Entertainment, 1999. Film.

one inconsequential man. As the movie continues, the Second Rangers did save Private Ryan, but most of the men who saved him died.

Saving Private Ryan is one of the most anti-cultural, anti-productive messages ever told, particularly today as numbers continue to prevail against personal relationships. As I watched it, the questions—would I have fired Judas or saved Private Ryan—ultimately intersected with my personal faith journey.

ORDERS

Why wouldn't Jesus fire Judas, and why would those soldiers save that stranger? Both of those stories have something in common: orders. Those soldiers were ordered to save Private Ryan and Jesus was sent to redeem the world by His Father:

> I have come down from heaven not to do my will but to do the will of him who sent me (John 6:38). In fact, for this reason I was born (John 18:37).

Those were their orders. And orders change everything. Or they should.

MISSION

Some understand this as a mission, even those in corporate America. In fact, best-selling author Steven Covey writes about this in *First Things First: To Live, to Love, to Learn, to Leave a Legacy.*[7] Many understand the importance of a corporate mission statement. It keeps organizations focused on their purpose. All successful companies know why they exist and what they are trying to achieve. Everyone needs a personal mission statement—an understanding of the reason we are on this earth.

A personal mission statement may not sound the same as orders. But for Christians, it just might be in the ballpark. And close enough to make the point. Those of us who believe in God know we have a Commanding Officer—our Creator. That is clear. Most of us are also well aware that the Bible implies He has a plan for our life. We often quote the following:

> "For I know the plans I have for you," declares the Lord, "plans to prosper and not to harm you, plans to give you hope and a future" (Jeremiah 29:11).

7. Covey, Stephen R., and A. Roger Merrill. *First Things First: To Live, to Love, to Learn, to Leave a Legacy.* New York: Simon & Schuster, 1994.

Furthermore, a study of biblical characters reveals that most of them were on a specific mission. Noah was called to build an ark; Abraham was called to leave his home and start a nation; Jonah was called to preach to Nineveh; Paul was called to preach to the Gentiles, and Peter to the Jews; and Jesus was called to die for the salvation of mankind. This list just names a few. There are many, many more. We also know of contemporary callings. Most would agree that Mother Teresa, Billy Graham, Rick Warren, and other prominent Christian leaders have been called to do the work they do.

So for us, our orders are the mission God has given us to fulfill on this earth, our purpose. And we all have "orders." Some of our orders are generic, like the fundamental call to love God and our neighbor as our self and to make disciples. Others are more specific, like the previous examples.

PERSONAL CALLING

I faced this crisis of *orders* years ago when I had to make a life-changing decision: marriage. I was engaged, and paralyzed with fear. The severity of this hit me when I heard a speaker say that most men die with their dreams still in them. He went on to discuss the importance of knowing your God-given "purpose." And I didn't. I wondered if I would be one of those regretful men. This became so important to me that I did the only thing I knew how to do to find clarity of purpose: I stopped eating for forty days.

I got the clarity I sought, at least enough to make the first step. I was called into a war on poverty, just like the soldiers in *Saving Private Ryan* had been called into the Second World War. I was to be a soldier in a war, the spiritual one raging behind the scenes of the reality we see every day. It's the war I discuss at length in my previous book, *Second Wind.*[8]

WHERE DO WE DISCOVER OUR CALLING?

It dawned on me that knowing one's God-given purpose, and obeying it, is critical to a healthy human being. Otherwise, we are grasping at cheap substitutes such as drugs, alcohol, sex, food, work, or worse, chasing the next carrot we think will make us happy. But without satisfying the thirst we have for *purpose*, we are merely surviving.

It is also critical for a healthy culture. What happens to us individually causes a domino effect in our culture. If enough of us are chasing after the wrong god, our entire culture will fall. Sound familiar? Turn on the news tonight and you will see the results of this. We need to recognize the effect

---

8. Wheeler, Thomas Alan. *Second Wind.* Oviedo, Florida: HigherLife, 2012.

of our choices on our culture, but unfortunately, most people don't. Instead people are caught up in the world—surviving, albeit comfortably in the United States—but often at the expense of our true *raison d'etre*—our most important purpose in life.

We need a place to discover our orders, have them affirmed (or challenged), and have other committed and trained soldiers walking with us while we live out our orders—despite the cost. That is what I needed anyway—which brings me to my own testimony from a lost soul to a model church member to an urban leader wondering how I got "here."

PART ONE

MY STORY

FROM A DISCIPLE
OF THE WORLD
TO A
DISCIPLE OF CHRIST
CALLED TO LOVE
HIS POOR

1

A Bite from the Forbidden Fruit

"Your time is limited, so don't waste it living someone else's life."
—Steve Jobs[9]

THE AMERICAN DREAM

I met Steve Jobs on Waikiki Beach just after having witnessed the introduction of Macintosh and the now famous "1984" commercial the evening before. Apple cofounder Jobs and John Sculley, Apple's CEO, were walking down the beach deep in conversation when I introduced myself. Meeting Steve Jobs and John Sculley was like meeting history before things became historical. I was twenty-three.

I worked for the firm representing Apple in the Washington, DC, area called RII Sales, named after R2D2 from *Star Wars*. RII Sales recruited me from Kramer Systems, Inc., a small computer firm that sold Intertec Super-Brain computers running DOS and Fortune Systems UNIX-based computers primarily to the federal government. RII offered me double the money I was making.

PARADISE

Within a month of being hired by RII Sales I was sent to paradise. I was in Waikiki, Hawaii, for the Apple Worldwide Sales Conference. I still have a vivid memory of stepping off the jet and smelling normal jet fumes mixed with the not-so-normal sweet aroma of fresh orchid leis. It was intoxicating, particularly when they put that sweetness around my neck. I was shuttled to the Hilton Hawaiian Village, one of the finest resorts in Waikiki. I had become connected to the American dream via this burgeoning company founded in a garage called Apple Computer. In a few short weeks my life had drastically changed. I was in heaven! Or so I thought.

PARTY

In Hawaii we spent most of our days learning about the Mac, reviewing

---

9. Jobs, Steve. "Stay Hungry. Stay Foolish." Lecture, 114th Commencement, Stanford University, June 12, 2005.

statistics on the computer industry and spending time understanding how to market the new Macintosh computer. Our nights were free to do as we pleased. And that meant drink, a lot. Mai Tais were the drink of preference while in paradise and most of us acted like kids in a candy store—no boundaries. Each morning everyone shared their wild escapades of the previous evening, laughing at some of the cruder things other Apple disciples had done. Everything was good. But I still had not found the highest "high" that I assumed I would find in paradise. To my surprise, on one of those nights I felt the same emptiness I experienced at home. I might have been in paradise but other than the incredible change in scenery, it didn't feel any different than Virginia. I had already had enough to drink one night, but I decided to have a few more at a local bar. Then a thought came to mind out of nowhere: run the tab, leave without paying.

RUN THE TAB

It wasn't about the money since Apple was picking up the tab; it was about doing something to relieve my boredom and challenge my being. Nervous as I was, I walked out without paying. To my surprise, it was noticed immediately and someone from the bar came running after me. Scared, I distanced myself from the fellow and instinctively intermingled with a local crowd of tourists roaming the open-air shops. Ditching the light jacket I had on allowed me to blend in with others, and the guy chasing me ran on by. I knew how to get away – instinctively. Certain I had avoided being caught, the adrenaline died down, and I felt relief and shock. It was over but what on earth had I been thinking?

WHAT WAS GOING ON?

Why was I risking the best job I had ever had for some adrenaline kick? I was used to drinking too much. I had done plenty of binge drinking in my college days, so that was nothing new. Unlike some who get mean and depressed, drinking made me happy, confident, and devious. Still, why risk the best thing that had happened to me for a challenge? Coinciding with these thoughts, the local news ran a story about a tourist who was involved in a fatal accident. He had driven his car off one of the steep Hawaiian cliffs. I remember thinking how unfortunate that would be: dying in paradise.

It seemed like a contradiction, but I connected it to my own circumstances. I understood that someone could die just as easily in Hawaii as anywhere else in the world, particularly if you lived as though you couldn't. And someone could just as easily be thrown into jail in Hawaii as they could anywhere else if they committed a crime, including me. How would I explain that I ran up a bill, and put someone else's room on the tab when I wasn't paying for my own anyway? Lie? Probably, yes. I would have lied. One sin leads to the next. Scary.

Apple sent me to Hawaii a half a dozen more times and it remains one of the most beautiful places I have ever been, but it was never the paradise I had thought it would be before I went. It was another glimpse that life was not going to work out the way I thought. I kept searching. A series of other incidents made me question whether I would ever find what I was looking for in the place I was looking—this world. This was to be my wake-up call. Watching the hypocrisy of the world intertwined with the darkness of my own life ultimately drove me back into the local church to see what I might have missed in my youth. Was there really a God? How could I know for sure? And where the heck was He if He did exist?

CHAPTER 1
QUESTIONS

1. What dream are you following?

2. Has your life worked out the way you thought it would?

3. What have you pursued in your life that led to a dead end?

4. Have you ever done something that made you wonder what you were thinking?

5. What did the world offer you before you became a Christian? If you are not a Christian, what does the world offer you now?

6. Are you ready to try a different path or have you already chosen one?

2 My Road to Damascus

"He is no fool who gives what he cannot keep to gain
that which he cannot lose."
—Jim Elliott

SUNDAY SCHOOL TEACHER

When I returned to church to see if I could make sense out of life, I could not understand what the minister was saying—although I heard the words. Having visited the church as a kid I knew its traditions, including our recital of the Lord's Prayer. One Sunday when we were reciting that prayer I wondered if anyone in the congregation actually knew why they were reciting it beyond pure rote. I sure didn't.

I considered standing up and asking that question out loud while we were praying, but decided that wouldn't go over too well. I doubted they understood it though, particularly because the prayer starts by saying "Our Father" and most people don't view God as their Father. I was offered a better option.

Later in the service the minister made a plea for a fifth-grade Sunday school teacher. He said they were the most challenging group of kids they had. Not knowing anything about the Bible but liking challenges, I accepted the call. I figured I might just get answers to the questions I was asking about life in doing this.

Surprisingly, they never asked me if I had any ability to teach or even if I was a believer. They just let me fill that hole in the church.

SHOCK

I bought a teen Bible, the New International Version, and began to read it. I was shocked. First, I was in shock because I understood what it said. Previously I had read the King James Version because I thought it was the *only version* of the Bible, but I could never understand it. Second, I was in shock because of what the Bible said: that God loved me despite anything I had ever done in my life, but that I was not living the way He intended and had to

23

stop. It touched on all of the points I had previously learned about life and people—mostly that people make lousy gods. I knew that no man could have written the Bible because what it teaches is the opposite of the way of the world. Only God, using inspired people, could have written the Bible. That was the end of my old life. I decided I would never again be against God. If God is for me, then I am for Him. My thirst for more kept me seeking Him at different depths.

FOLLOWING WHAT I KNEW

In Alexandria, Virginia, I never recall having heard about being "born again," but I had come to realize that following God was the only way to live life. And I was following Him as best I knew how. It reminds me of the story of Cornelius the centurion in the book of Acts.[10] Cornelius was serving God but didn't know Jesus as Lord and Savior until Peter came to his house and told him exactly who He was.

I moved to Charlotte and was invited to attend Forest Hill Church by a friend. I had never experienced church the way I did at Forest Hill. Everything about it was refreshing for someone new in his faith: the people, the worship music, and the relevant preaching and teaching. I felt like I was finally home. In one of the first sermons I heard there, Pastor David Chadwick preached John 3:3 from the pulpit:

> In reply Jesus declared, "I tell you the truth, no one can see the kingdom of God unless he is born again" (John 3:3).

BORN-AGAINERS

I had been raised to believe that the "born-againers," as they were called in my family, were religious nuts who should be kept at a distance. My mom later told me the reason she felt that way was because she had never heard about being born again in church, ever, so it seemed strange to her. Because of my parents' apparent disdain for those who considered themselves "born again," I did not want to be one of them. As the third kid in my family I had learned to submit, and getting along with people was important to me. But the path I was on was going against the grain of just about everyone in my life. I was becoming an oddball, and that has always been difficult for me. As a chubby kid nicknamed "doughboy" I had learned at a young age how mean people could be, particularly kids. But once I heard John 3:3 preached I believed

---

10. Acts 10.

what it said. I accepted the truth and submitted my life to Jesus Christ as my Lord and Savior. The Bible says:

> If you declare with your mouth, "Jesus is Lord," and believe in your heart that God raised him from the dead, you will be saved (Romans 10:9).

I made that declaration and became a follower of the Jesus I had always heard about but never knew. I became a born-again Christian.

MDC

By this time I had cofounded a company of my own called Multimedia Design Corporation (MDC). Designers of educational software, we struggled to keep up with the growing multimedia industry. That meant we were always undercapitalized, a typical problem for many companies. We raised a couple million dollars but it was never enough. My business partner, previously a restaurateur, had also become very knowledgeable about the computer industry. His ability to lead the company was now similar to mine. And I was different.

I remember him telling me he wanted the old Tom Wheeler back since the new one was not as pushy as the old one. I know many people misunderstand those who have life-changing events like mine but, for those of us who have had them, we know it is not like turning a switch on and off at will. There is a power far greater than ours, inside of us, driving us, guiding us. This caused division between my partner and me. I ended up leaving the company. Already involved with Forest Hill, I was offered an internship to work with them on a part-time basis. I accepted. Now I was working at the church I had come to love—the bride of Christ.

FHC AND SEMINARY

I heard critics say that nobody could be sure of what the Bible said because of translation issues, that it could be interpreted many different ways. There were very many schools of thought about biblical concepts. Some even said there were mistakes in the Bible. After looking at various seminaries, I enrolled in a local one, Gordon-Conwell Theological Seminary, to get a better understanding of the Bible. The church supported my enrollment and agreed to pay for my tuition, something I have always been grateful for, since I could not have done it without their full support. The church continued to be "the church" to me.

In seminary I studied the Bible's authenticity. I studied it to understand what it said, why it said it, what was meant by what it said, as well as translation issues that might impact the true meaning of what we read today, and whether it was true that the Bible was (and is) interpretable by the individual. This solidified my faith.

FOCUS ON THE ESSENTIALS

I found there were things in the Bible that were difficult to understand, but nothing I learned rendered the essential elements of the Bible subject to individual interpretation. It was not any different than accounting practices: the basics were constant, just like two plus two equals four. The Bible says this about the apostle Paul's contributions to the Bible:

> His letters contain some things that are hard to understand, which ignorant and unstable people distort, as they do the other Scriptures, to their own destruction (2 Peter 3:16).

But looking around at Christians today, I do understand why so many think the Bible is subject to the individual's interpretation. Many professed Christians live a life in direct contradiction of the Bible's teachings—the very same teachings they say they believe. Even in the church there is disagreement over parts of the Bible or the way to live out your faith. That is why there are so many denominations. While this did not impact my own faith, it did cause me to stay away from those who focused on the trivial over the essentials. It also showed me the importance of not missing the truth in the midst of all the opinions. I tried not to major on the minors.

INTERN

As an intern at my church my supervisor and mentor gave me the opportunity to lead the singles group. He also gave me lots of opportunities to teach, which I discovered was one of my top spiritual gifts and passions. Additionally, I was in a small group of men, so I had a safe place to share my life and make disciples. I developed a close relationship with another fellow from the group who became my accountability partner in response to the Scripture in James:

> Therefore confess your sins to each other and pray for each other so that you may be healed. The prayer of a righteous man is powerful and effective (James 5:16).

Eventually I became an elder. The church had become my family and the singles group my support system. Some staff members even began to refer to me as the *model* of what they were hoping would happen to everyone in the church. I had committed my life to Jesus. I had given up my old lifestyle, and become fully engaged in His work, at the expense of my own. I had also begun teaching others to do the same. I was a new man, and anyone who knew me before knew that was true.

CHAPTER 2
QUESTIONS

1. Do you believe the Bible is subject to individual interpretation? If so, do you believe that about all areas or only the ones you consider minor? How do you know you are following God's standard?

2. What do you think it means to be "born again"?

3. Do you consider your church to be your family?

4. Has the Devil done anything in your life that is keeping you from fulfilling your God-given destiny?

3

Learning to "Be" While Pushed to "Do"

"We are human beings. We don't want to be fixed. We want
to be respected, loved, appreciated, needed and understood.
When this happens, we are in a position to be transformed."
—Author

GROUPS

Then the church hired me as the Assistant Director of Discipleship in charge
of the membership class as well as developing small cell groups, a movement
that is now popular across the country. The church understood the importance of members connecting with one another, that discipleship mattered
and getting folks into groups was their answer to how the discipleship process
would work. It was my job to connect people into ministry, in both groups
and service. And I did. But while doing this, I began to notice how busy we
were making our already busy members. Coincidentally I read a book at that
time by Dr. Larry Crabb called *Connecting: Healing for Ourselves and Our
Relationships: A Radical New Vision.*[11]

CONNECTING

In his book Dr. Crabb shares a compelling argument about our need to stop
"doing Christianity" and to start living it in community with other believers.
He mentions a story about someone he had counseled for some time. Months
after the counseling had ended, Dr. Crabb ran into his former client. He
asked him what his client remembered most about the counseling sessions he
had provided. The man said it was the time he had seen Dr. Crabb outside
of counseling and talked with him like they were friends, rather than in their
counselor/patient capacity. It was not one of his counseling sessions.

Jim Kalam says in *Risking Church*:

"If we can't release churches to become communities, our spiritual
growth is at risk. We'll become fish out of water; we'll be creatures
made for water, dying in the desert."[12]

---

11. Crabb, Larry. *Connecting: Healing for Ourselves and Our Relationships: A Radical New Vision.* Nashville,
Tenn.: Word Pub., 1997.
12. Kalam, Jr., Jim. *Risking Church.* Charlotte, NC: Kalam Press, 2003. 31.

We are human beings. We don't want to be fixed. We want to be respected, loved, appreciated, needed and understood. When this happens, we are in a position for God to transform us. While the small group model affirmed what my church was implementing, it still provoked me to create a pie chart of the average member's time, including our expectations of our members. I charted things such as family time, church on Sunday and Wednesdays (when we had a Wednesday night service), time with our real neighbors, small-group time, serving time, individual quiet time, as well as the obvious things such as work, sleep, time eating, and free time.

HUMAN "DOERS"

When I got done looking at the pie chart of the typical person's time, starting with my own (and I was single), there didn't seem to be much margin in the lives of the people we were asking to get more involved in the work of our grace-oriented church. Small groups just added to their already busy schedule. It wasn't the group model that was problematic to me. Most people agreed that groups were necessary to be part of the DNA of the church; it was the fact that the groups were just one aspect of the "model." When was Jesus ever "busy" the way we were? While Jesus didn't put Martha down, he did encourage her to be more like Mary:

> As Jesus and his disciples were on their way, he came to a village where a woman named Martha opened her home to him. She had a sister called Mary, who sat at the Lord's feet listening to what he said. But Martha was distracted by all the preparations that had to be made. She came to him and asked, "Lord, don't you care that my sister has left me to do the work by myself? Tell her to help me!" "Martha, Martha," the Lord answered, "you are worried and upset about many things, but few things are needed —or indeed only one. Mary has chosen what is better, and it will not be taken away from her" (Luke 10:38-42).

WHY DID WE SEEM TO BE FOLLOWING MARTHA?

Furthermore, just because someone was in a group didn't always translate into discipleship. Because it was my job, I made it my responsibility to know what was happening in some of these groups and I found it was not the kind of discipleship that was life-transforming. We might have looked good on paper, but the reality was that many of the groups were just social gatherings of lukewarm Christians. I wanted to reorganize the groups, but my supervisor stressed to me that my primary job was to get members into a group, not reduce the groups over quality control, although he too understood the issue. I saw that as a problem that I believe still exists in many churches. For those members that were hot for Christ, reaching out in the workplace, in their neighborhoods, to their families, and maybe even to the people they exercised with, we were just adding fuel to the fire of burnout.

JESUS HAD TWELVE

Since I believed in a relational discipleship process, one that teaches what Jesus taught using my example and my words, I understood that in order to disciple the group leaders I was going to have to spend a lot more time with them than I had been. This was also when my twelve (Jesus trained twelve men to carry on His work) grew to over 100. I presented a report expressing my concern to the leadership, without much of a response. I noticed that the leaders of my church were leading groups of others, sometimes multiple groups, but not all of them were in a group with each other. The "iron sharpening iron" (Proverbs 27:17) principle was not engaged as much as I had thought. Some were in a group, but I found out later they were too busy to consistently meet. I also knew of situations with leadership that did not seem to be reconciled because of what appeared to be a lack of time. It was not a lack of concern: all the leaders in my church were concerned with one another—it was a lack of depth in their relationship. One longtime staff member of the church announced his resignation and was gone in a manner more conducive to a Fortune 500 company than a church. Another one of the leaders committed adultery and ended up in jail. Several other leaders of the church left in a huff. Without trying to judge or assume, I made a mental note that I may be more sensitive in my assessment about margin than most. Still, I trusted my leaders to make changes as the Lord led them.

MOTHER TERESA

The more I read and studied the Bible, the more I was attracted to the poor. That included studying Mother Teresa and her work. I heard criticism from some who said Mother Teresa was not a Christian, but when I looked at her life and compared her life to her critics and then to Jesus, her life resembled the Jesus I had come to know. She was known as one of the most loving people on the planet, and the Bible says God is love (1 John 4:16). How could she be so full of love if she were not following God, I wondered? She simply lived out her faith and total dependence on Jesus through her deeds, rather than many of us who did it through words. In a world fighting for success, she was satisfied to be faithful without concern about worldly success—something very few people understand, even knowing her miraculous story. She was (and is) ignored as an anomaly, rather than revered as a model. But not by me. I noticed.

LIVING FAITH

My church leaders were constantly preaching about the need for Christians to help the poor. Listening very intently each Sunday, I had difficulty passing the men and women I saw on the street corner holding signs for support. I knew all of the stereotypes about them, too: they were lazy, criminals, drug addicts, or drunks who deserved what they were getting because they caused their homelessness. But I began to have doubts. I decided to stop and talk to the homeless people I saw and ask them why they weren't in a shelter. Most told me the shelters were full of drugs and other criminal activity so they remained on the streets. That is why they needed so much of my help. For some time I bought that line. I took in a homeless man and his dog during a snowstorm. I met others on the streets whom I helped, as well.

MATTHEW 25:40

Then a Scripture that has become one of my life verses jumped off the page while I was reading it:

> Whatever you did for one of the least of these brothers and sisters of mine, you did for me (Matthew 25:40).

Another section of Scripture stuck as well: the one about the rich man and Lazarus (Luke16:19-31). Lazarus was a beggar who laid at the gate of a rich man who paid no attention to him. Then they both died. Angels carried the poor man, Lazarus, to Abraham in heaven while the rich man landed in hell because of his negligence regarding Lazarus. That stuck, too. If we consider ourselves Christian, we need to help the poor. But how?

CHAPTER 3
QUESTIONS

1. How much time do you have in your day when you can just relax?

2. On the next page take a moment to fill in the pie chart of a typical 24-hour day of yours and plot the following:
   Time spent working at your job or vocation
   Time sleeping
   Time exercising
   Time praying
   Time eating
   Time reading the Bible
   Time relaxing
   Time being entertained or just having fun
   Time spent with your family
   Time spent serving others (even if just 'listening' to your neighbor)
   Time sharing your faith with others
   Time spent building relationships as a mentor
   Time spent receiving from a mentor
   Time spent in a discipleship relationship with another person

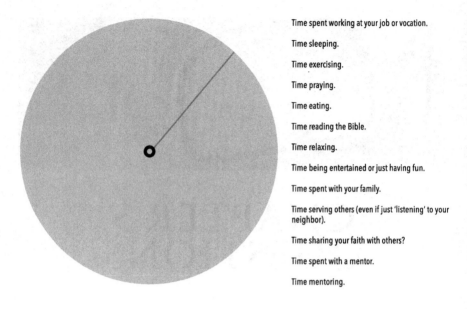

Time spent working at your job or vocation.

Time sleeping.

Time exercising.

Time praying.

Time eating.

Time reading the Bible.

Time relaxing.

Time being entertained or just having fun.

Time spent with your family.

Time serving others (even if just 'listening' to your neighbor).

Time sharing your faith with others?

Time spent with a mentor.

Time mentoring.

4. Based upon your pie chart what are your top ten priorities?

1.

2.

3.

4.

5.

6.

7.

8.

9.

10.

4 Affirmed to Be a Missionary to the Poor

Time Magazine: What is God's greatest gift to you?
Mother Teresa: The poor people.
Time: How are they a gift?
Mother Teresa: I have an opportunity to be with Jesus 24 hours a day.[13]

REVELATION 3:15

Over time I got comfortable. I couldn't tell you exactly what happened except to say I started to adapt back into my culture. That is when I went on the forty-day fast to deal with the demons of my past, including the incident in Hawaii, and to understand why on earth I was here. It all began with a dream.

> I know your deeds, that you are neither cold nor hot. I wish you were either one or the other! (Revelation 3:15)

THE DREAM

In my dream Michael Jordan and I were walking together down a sidewalk in a peaceful but unknown place. I was sharing the gospel with him as he looked straight ahead, never making eye contact with me, as if making the subtle but dreamlike point that I did not know him. During our short "dream walk" he told me not to forget Revelation 3:15. Then we swapped hats; I took his and he took mine. And I woke up.

Believing dreams can have meaning I grabbed my Bible to see what Revelation 3:15 said. It was an eye-opener. God was telling the complacent church in Laodicea to be hot or cold, but not lukewarm; evidently their wealth had blinded them to their true spirituality. It made me seriously consider my life, particularly because the next verse, Revelation 3:16, said God will spit lukewarm Christians out of His mouth. Ouch. It wasn't the easiest message to hear, but was I lukewarm? I was on staff at my church! Lukewarm? Me? Really?

13. Teresa, Mother. "A Pencil in the Hand of God." Interview by Edward W. Desmond for Time magazine. December 4, 1989.

LUKEWARM? ME?

With my history? I used to work for Apple, started my own company, had my own Cessna airplane, flew helicopters, and lived on the water. I had given up that lifestyle for Jesus. Once I had even given away all my savings, after suggesting some rich guy do the same before he committed suicide, as he was threatening to do. He wouldn't do it, but I felt challenged. Could I practice what I was preaching? So I did it. How could I be lukewarm? Maybe this dream was meant for someone else and I was given it by mistake! But I knew God didn't make mistakes. And why did God have Michael Jordan delivering this message to me, I wondered? I had never met Michael Jordan, but like most of us I knew who he was: the greatest basketball player of all time. Perhaps God used Michael Jordan in my dream because He wanted me to get the message to be hot for Christ from someone who was the best in his field. Regardless of any other theory, reason, or possibility, that is the message I got: be on fire for Christ like Michael Jordan was on fire for basketball. Stay focused. Persevere. Never quit. But what did that mean, exactly?

ST. CROIX OR THE SHELTER

Coincidentally, during the same time frame I was planning to swim in a five-mile race in St. Croix, Virgin Islands. A couple of weeks before the race I was driving alone in my car and felt compelled to ask God a question. "God," I asked, "where will You be while I am swimming in this race in St. Croix?" I asked that question knowing that God is omnipresent (therefore, always with me), but thinking He might just give me an answer that would appease my apprehension about taking this vacation after having that dream. You know the answer I mean, that God will be with me wherever I go because He loves me so much; therefore, stay the course, go swim the swim. It's our way of justifying whatever we want to do because "God loves us." But that is not the answer I heard. Instantly I heard these words:

"I'll be at the Uptown Men's Shelter."

Oh, my. Really? There?

I canceled my trip to St. Croix and checked myself into that same shelter as a homeless man. I stayed there for four days to be with Jesus—the same amount of time I would have been in St. Croix living in a five-star hotel and swimming in that race. Nobody knew me as anything but "one of them"—homeless.

SHELTER

The shelter wasn't the Holiday Inn but it was far nicer than its critics said it was. While there I quickly learned the plight of the poor was not like my stereotypes. Some were, of course, but it is funny how different people are to us when we get to know their real story. I saw the beauty of the men, most of whom had lived lives that caused me to ask the question: if I had walked in their shoes, where would I be? I recalled my own past and stories. I just hadn't been caught for some of the bad things I had done. But what if I had?

Of course there were the con artists too, but for the most part the men were genuine and really delightful people. Once, in the middle of the night as I tried to sleep in the midst of the stench, the bodily sounds, and the feeling that small creatures were crawling all over me in the bed where I slept, a dim light from the men's room hit two men who were talking, morphing them into giants when their shadows hit the wall where I was looking. One of those men was proclaiming the life, death, and resurrection of Jesus to an attentive listener. I don't know how else to explain it. I felt as though I were watching Jesus proclaim the truth of His being to this other homeless man. In the midst of my physical discomfort living in the shelter—I saw that. *Jesus really was in the shelter.*

AFFIRMED

This was also the time I had extensive Christian counseling in an effort to let God heal me of my past. There was more healing to come, I would discover, but this was the beginning. I went on a few more overseas mission trips and volunteered my time each week feeding the homeless at The Harvest Center in Charlotte, a part of Community Outreach Church, led by the Reverend Barbara Brewton Cameron. I was exposed to some of the poorest people in the world. Through a process of discovery, I was sure God was calling me to love His poor in my city. I was to help the homeless. Being a church-abiding person under the authority of my church, I approached my pastor and asked what he thought about my calling to the poor. I needed his affirmation to take a step toward my calling. I was a member of his flock, and he was one of the most respected men I knew. He also knew my journey toward the poor. Several years before I had done a report on the homeless for the sake of a wealthy man who wanted to eliminate homelessness in Charlotte. I had been asked to help. The report I came up with suggested the best way to help the poor was to support the plethora of organizations already helping the poor. That was not the answer the man wanted to hear. But it helped my pastor to know more about me. He also knew I had fasted for forty days for clarification of my calling during a difficult time in my life. He affirmed my call.

Next I asked the "Session" of my church, its governing body, for their blessing. As an elder myself I felt it important to have their affirmation. They unanimously affirmed my call as well. I was sent out in a way much like an international missionary but in my own backyard.

> Obey your spiritual leaders and do what they say. Their work is to watch over your souls, and they are accountable to God (Hebrews 13:17—NLT).

WORKING AT THE SHELTER

I resigned my position at the church and accepted a job at the Uptown Men's Shelter as a first step to my own call. Because I was only making $10 per hour as an entry-level supervisor, the pastor in charge of missions began to financially support me from his budget. I also began looking for a place to live in what some call "the hood" since I couldn't afford my south Charlotte house and I wanted to be immersed in my calling. Internationally known civil rights leader John Perkins and Robert (Bob) Lupton, founder of FCS Urban Ministries in Atlanta, Georgia, who developed two mixed-income subdivisions by moving into the inner city of Atlanta, believe those who want to help the poor need to move in with them. They believe this is the best answer to mending the challenges we have working with the poor. That is when I met Johnny Allen. Johnny told me he lived in the Hoskins/Thomasboro neighborhood in northwest Charlotte and invited me to stop by and check it out. I did.

HOSKINS/THOMASBORO

The Hoskins area is a couple of miles from the epicenter of Charlotte, North Carolina, and typically defined by high crime, poverty, low education, unemployment, and substandard housing.[14] Johnny moved into the Hoskins area in 2001. He immediately began moving the homeless into his rented house under the informally organized ministry he had created called Jesus Anointed Ministries (JAM). I moved in as Johnny's neighbor on Easter Sunday, 2002.

I took men into my home, just like Johnny was doing, either because the shelter was full or because they were no longer eligible to stay there. The first person I took in was a seventy-year-old African-American man named Al who was on his way to sleep in a broken-down school bus as I was going home

---

14. "Point2 Homes." Charlotte Demographics & Statistics. Accessed October 20, 2015.

from my shift at the shelter. He said he had been banned from the shelter because he didn't follow their rules. But he was seventy and it was late. Al was my first roommate.

The second housemate was a twenty-something African American named Montel. He was a very well-mannered guy who eventually stole my neighbor's purse, ringing up hundreds of dollars of phone fees before he disappeared. The third fellow was Todd, a wonderful thirty-something-year-old man who was a full-time force to be reckoned with.

AGAINST POLICY

Unbeknownst to me, taking the homeless into my own house was against the policy of my employer, the Uptown Men's Shelter. In an effort to comply with their rules I had the men living with me find another place. The shelter, however, in a mysterious set of political circumstances, said they had accepted my resignation and after working at the shelter for nearly a year, I found myself without a job. I turned to my church but leadership had transitioned. I had assumed Johnny would welcome me with open arms. And he did, theoretically speaking that is. But the reality of our journey was quite different. Johnny was working with another fellow who had served as a mentor to Johnny and who didn't want my help.

HOSKINS PARK

In response I founded Hoskins Park Ministries on November 19, 2002, under another company called The National Heritage Foundation (NHF). It had not been my plan to start a ministry to the poor; I was simply responding to the circumstances I was in. And I was now the head of a *parachurch* organization. I go into this at a deeper level in chapter 10, but for now, a parachurch organization is one that is organized outside the typical church structure and devoted to a particular cause like I was. Connecting with NHF allowed me to quickly get nonprofit status for those who might want to make a tax-free donation to the cause I was now involved with: helping the homeless.

And the donations came. I had several friends who knew what I was doing and supported me. One man in particular gave me enough that I did not have to be concerned about money. From the beginning, Hoskins Park was funded because of this handful of people. Using NHF, all of my financial information was recorded, all bills paid, and the organization was legally authorized to operate. But for all practical purposes, I was without the body of Christ.

CHAPTER 4
QUESTIONS

1. What Scriptures have impacted you enough to redirect your life?

2. What is your definition of poverty?

3. According to the way the world defines poverty, was Jesus poor? How about Paul?

4. Does that change your view of poverty (or homeless people)?

5. Have you been on an overseas short-term mission trip? How did it impact you?

5 My Private Ryan

"If your theology is not your biography,
then your theology is worthless."
—David and Jason Benham[15]

JA MINISTRIES

Meanwhile Johnny was doing his work under the name of his ministry, JA Ministries. Johnny made the men work, charged them $100 per week for rent and had Bible study and prayer time each day. Johnny kept no records and JA Ministries was never incorporated.

At different times we would discuss the men we were both caring for since we were trying to work together, but we had difficulty agreeing on how they should be treated. In my case I had guys whom I did not require to work when Johnny thought they should. Johnny had guys using drugs and still living with him who I thought he should let go. And while I had to learn from Johnny that we should not kick guys out for what brought them in, Johnny knew he was letting some of them stay longer than they should because they were paying rent and he needed the money. Since I was funded at the time, that was not an issue for me or for Hoskins Park Ministries. I was focused on the growth and development of the men even though I had no idea how to really help them through such a process. I was more of an enabler. As a result, we both ended up with distinct and individual ministries serving the poor.

OPPOSITES ATTRACT

Coming from a fairly healthy middle-class family, having a graduate education, and having successfully worked for a Fortune 500 company, I am organized and get things done professionally, for the most part. Appearance matters to me, right and wrong are typically important, and doing things legally is required. I turned my life over to Jesus Christ when I got most of the things I thought would make me happy but didn't. Johnny, my partner-to-be, came from a broken family living in poverty, didn't have a father and actually

---

15. "Whatever the Cost." In Touch.org. July 3, 2015. Accessed September 25, 2015.

had to become one to his seven brothers and sisters at the age of thirteen. Johnny had to be his own dad. Furthermore, his education was inhibited by his circumstances. Eventually he got involved in drugs, became a drug dealer, spent time in jail, and ended up homeless. After he had enough of that life, he turned his life over to Jesus Christ and was brought to a Christian shelter similar to what we founded at Hoskins Park.

DIFFERENT BACKGROUNDS, SAME CALLING

I don't know if Johnny was a born leader or not, but because of his life he had to become one in order to survive. Furthermore, Johnny had hands-on experience with the homeless population both through his own experiences and because he actually worked for the organization that helped him, Mission Corps. He understood how to deal with men in poverty. I did not.

I had the organizational experience having worked at Apple and having started my own business. I knew how to put things in right order. That is why I wanted to come storming in with my experiences as an entrepreneur, my professional ideas, my Christianity, and my to-do lists: to improve Johnny and the way he was doing things. But that approach didn't work.

I thought I knew enough about people and the Bible to help Johnny do the part where he was most gifted even better. Johnny felt he was qualified to run the organization well enough his way. Coming from completely different cultures, we had a surface-level relationship.

RESPECT

I was focused on what Johnny was *doing* rather than loving him for who he was. He was doing the same thing with me. *We were each a means to an end.* We were living the corporate business model. But that method caused constant friction and frustration between us. Sometimes we got so angry that one of us would stomp out of the room to cool down. Thankfully, the Lord allowed a third person, Doug Taylor, to arbitrate between us as a peacemaker, even though sometimes Doug would get caught in the mix just like Johnny and I. I can laugh about it now but back then it was not so funny—it was just plain hard. Trusting in God to work through people is easier said than done.

JOHNNY AND I

Johnny and I were trying to work together but still butting heads because of the way we approached the work. We were trying to help one another and let each other do what we do best, individually, but our worlds were far apart, something that I would learn much more about later. One day we were sitting in front of a spreadsheet discussing some numbers. They were off. My spreadsheet had added the numbers differently than Johnny had. I pointed it out in order to make the correction. In my world a spreadsheet is the same as having a calculator. But Johnny felt challenged and we butted heads.

MERGE

He went to his house and I went back to mine. We were both incredibly frustrated. Then I went over to his house to apologize for my part in our argument. I also told him I was not going to do this work if this was the way we were going to deal with fairly simple matters. In fact, I said, if it happened again, I wouldn't keep doing this—a prophetic statement I would come to find out years later. He agreed. He mentioned his difficulty when someone challenged him because he had been put down so much in his life. As the third kid in my family, I was used to criticism too, but I was raised in a completely different manner than Johnny. Our cultures were clashing, even though I had no idea what that meant at the time. Finally, *after four years of living life together*, growing and maturing in our faith, and about the time I was ready to pack up and move out of the inner city (demographically speaking), and call it quits, the Lord spoke to me about Johnny. *Until I loved and thus respected* Johnny for who he was and what he did, nothing would change. Until I started focusing on how great a man Johnny was, accentuating the positive while modeling the areas in Johnny's life that I felt were my areas of strength (and his weaknesses), he was never going to trust me to support him: *I was simply another critic* and he'd had enough of those already.

AFFIRM

So every chance I got I started to let Johnny know how much he meant to me and that I could not and would not do this work without being in partnership with him. Over and over I told him this until he started to admit that he too needed the gifts God had given me in order to do the work even better than he already was. We learned to respect one another. More time passed until we began listening to each other, understanding each other a bit better. We decided to merge our two ministries into one in 2006 and called it Hoskins Park Ministries since I had already incorporated Hoskins Park and received nonprofit status from the IRS. I still felt it imperative for the long-term success of Hoskins Park to have a church partner. I may have been naive about poverty but I still thought that with the help of the local church, a committed army, this could work. This would prove to be one of my first tests working with Johnny because, while I believed in the local church, like many other urban leaders working with the poor, he did not.

CHAPTER 5
QUESTIONS

1. Can you relate to my experience in partnering with a grass-roots leader?

2. Do you believe your job (if you work) is primarily about the work you do or the people you meet?

3. How different would your life look if you focused more on the people you work with rather than the work itself?

4. Do you have your job to support a lifestyle, or because you love it, or because you feel you are called to do what you do?

6 Pursuing a Local Church Partner

"For just as each of us has one body with many members, and these members do not all have the same function, so in Christ we, though many, form one body, and each member belongs to all the others" (Romans 12:4-5).

NEXT CHURCH

I had been bringing the homeless guys from the ministry to my church. But they felt uncomfortable. My church had an affluent body and, right or wrong, these guys felt out of place. In order to support the men's desire to fit in and to get our ministry covered by the local church, which meant attending a church as a group, I sought out another church. I had heard about one that was more diverse and hoped our men might feel more comfortable. We tried it and everyone liked it, including a reluctant Johnny. (I later found out it wasn't that Johnny did not think a church needed to be involved in Hoskins Park but he had never experienced a church helping the way I said they would.) I was convinced it was just a matter of time before we connected with the right church.

THE RIGHT FIT

I introduced myself to the senior pastor of the new church and invited him to visit Hoskins Park to see what we were doing. He was on-site within a week. I was ecstatic. I explained to him how our ministry had evolved, the struggles we faced, and why I felt we needed the local church to be involved with Hoskins to a fairly substantial degree. He had experience with urban ministry work, agreed with my assessment that we needed a church, believed strongly that God intended to change the world through the local church and appeared to understand our struggles. This seemed to be just what we needed. Attending this new church each Saturday night became standard for everyone at Hoskins Park. Finally, we had a church. Or so we thought.

NEEDY CONGREGATION

While the church appreciated the work, and while their senior pastor completely understood our need for a church partnership to walk with us, it takes time to develop a partnership that is financially supported. At least that is what I was told. It is my strong belief that financial support accompanies discipleship in a true partnership. Leaders explained the financial support would come but over time since their benevolence budget could not keep up with their needy congregation. I was told that their congregation as a whole was fairly poor, so getting funds to pay existing expenses was difficult, unlike other "wealthier" churches in the area. As an experienced businessman I understood the reality of what the pastor said and trusted his explanation. I also trusted God to provide that which we needed. Meanwhile the financial burdens of the work at Hoskins Park grew larger since Hoskins was maturing as an organization.

GROWTH

Anyone who has started any organization from scratch knows there are stages of development and all of those stages require resources. If those resources do not come, the organization can become stagnant or fold like 80-85 percent of all start-up organizations.[16] The standards that apply to business[17] start-ups apply to the millions of church/parachurch start-ups as well.[18] Objectives and strategies must shift to meet the reality of these operations. One cannot manage an organization with ten people the same as one can manage an organization with 50, 100, 1,000, etc. Numbers change things. Period. Just ask Moses:

> What you are doing is not good. You and these people who come to you will only wear yourselves out. The work is too heavy for you; you cannot handle it alone. Select capable men from all the people—men who fear God, trustworthy men who hate dishonest gain—and appoint them as officials over thousands, hundreds, fifties and tens (Exodus 18:13-14, 17-25).

If the leaders of the organization do not develop along with the organization, they typically need to be replaced. But that option was not a viable one

16. Although not specifically distinguishing parachurches from churches. See White, James Emery. "Enrichment Journal—Enriching and Equipping Spirit-filled Ministers." Why New Churches Fail. 2015. Accessed September 29, 2015.
17. Wagner, Eric T. "Five Reasons 8 Out Of 10 Businesses Fail." Forbes. September 12, 2013. Accessed September 29, 2015.
18. "National Center for Charitable Statistics New." National Center for Charitable Statistics New. Accessed September 29, 2015.

to me because of the issue of calling and discipleship. I was called to disciple these leaders.

MATURING

Hoskins was maturing out of the start-up phase as we had grown to 13 houses, 60 men, a staff of eight and a budget nearing $500,000, but needed a lot more support than we were receiving in order to continue to mature in a healthy manner. I was becoming all too familiar with the difficulty of working with the homeless and our need to have a lot more "soldiers" helping us. Without them, I felt we were in over our heads with the work. We looked good to outsiders, but inside we were becoming overwhelmed. That puts leaders at risk of attack. The enemy does not play fair and helping the homeless requires an army—a united army. The church did not offer local urban leaders such as me weekly Bible study in a permanent discipleship process; instead, they had a process that was temporary. All the other urban leaders I knew were struggling for the same reasons; this was not about Hoskins Park, this was about our "industry," which we will discuss in a later chapter—an industry that either focuses on the leaders' performance at the expense of the leaders' Christian maturity or that focuses on the leaders maturity at the expense of the ministry itself.

UNABLE TO HELP

We waited patiently, even after hearing that the church had put aside some $200,000 to use for local ministry work but without giving it to the local ministries in their body, like Hoskins Park. Then they began a building campaign to raise $4 million. I was stunned. It was not the building campaign that caught me off guard; most churches do that, and I understand the need to develop their organization just like we do. Who was I to judge? What bothered me was the fact they had always told me they could not take care of their current flock, which was why they could not support us at a higher level. Now they were growing that same needy body at a cost of $4 million. And still without additional support for Hoskins. I recalled the time my home church had funded an urban church in Charlotte *before* they built their own facility. That had felt right. I brought my concerns to the leadership, but they had made up their minds to build.

CHURCH

One weekend they asked their congregation to give above the normal tithe for the building campaign. The next weekend the church announced they had raised $350,000 that previous weekend. That was the knockout punch. For the first time in my Christian life I felt out of place —in church. Despite their explanations, the work at Hoskins was clearly not a priority of theirs, and neither was I. This was made clear when I asked one of the senior leaders about it. Using my own metaphor, I asked if the church "knew their children." I was told emphatically, "You are not one of our children."

OUR KIDS

Healthy parents are cheerful about the support they give *their kids* because they are their kids. They don't make their kids beg for support and adoption. But if they do not consider someone their own, everything changes. That had been the point I was trying to make when I asked if we were one of the church's children. Given the church is a "parent" to its flock, if they truly know their kids, they work with them to understand their needs and help them. But we were not considered one of their kids; we were not truly a part of their body. That was the end of that.

The same church started an in-house outreach to the poor. They never told us. Then they stopped their Saturday night service in which our guys felt comfortable. Each time I mentioned my concerns to the leaders they had their own reasoning as to why they had to do these things. What happened? Where had I gone wrong? Had I misunderstood the mission of the church? Was I wrong about how a parachurch organization should interact with a church ministry? Had the church misunderstood their role? Or was this my "thorn in the flesh?" (2 Corinthians 12:7). Irrespective of how, I was on my own again—with no desire to be.

CHAPTER 6
QUESTIONS

1. Do you think the church is a "business"? If so, how so? If not, why not? What makes it different?

2. Do you think church "shopping" was invented by God or man? How does the average person decide what church to attend? How do you feel about that?

3. What is your process for deciding whom to give your money to, including the church?

4. What process does your church have for deciding whom to support? If you don't know, consider looking into it.

5. Do you know how much your church gives to specific organizations?

7 The Value of a Person

Oskar Schindler: "Look, all you have to do is tell me what it's worth to you. What's a person worth to you?"
Amon Goeth: "No, no, no, no. What's one worth to you?"[19]

WE ARE ALL PRIVATE RYAN TO SOMEONE

I continued to work with Johnny and encourage his own growth as a leader despite the obstacles we faced in not having the kind of church partner I expected. Then I started to wonder if God was more interested in me assisting Johnny to lead the work instead of Johnny helping me to be its leader. Was this about the biblical discipleship of *one man*? Was Johnny my version of Private Ryan? I was the Executive Director of Hoskins Park Ministries but I understood that the ministry could not grow faster than Johnny's ability to run the program. I originally moved in next to Johnny to help him with the work; I never wanted to do this on my own. As more time passed I was certain that Johnny was the point of everything. While helping the multitude of homeless people is a wonderful calling, mine was to love one formerly homeless man named Johnny, so that he could become his best. *My orders were about a person, not a cause.*

ORDERS

God would take care of the multitudes if I would take care of Johnny. Discipleship. True, biblical discipleship, the kind that requires lots of time and lots of love, had to be modeled at the top of Hoskins Park Ministries in order to filter through the whole ministry. God called Christians to disciple men rather than to fix or save them.

> Therefore go and make disciples of all nations, baptizing them in the name of the Father and of the Son and of the Holy Spirit, and teaching them to obey everything I have commanded you. And surely I am with you always, to the very end of the age (Matthew 28:19-20).

---

19. *Schindler's List* (R). Directed by Steven Spielberg. MCA/Universal Home Video, 1993. Film.

Discipleship at this level was far more difficult than building an organization. It required submission and sacrifice at a level that demanded more patience than many have or are willing to give. I was finding out just what the Bible meant when it said:

Better a patient person than a warrior, one with self-control than one who takes a city (Proverbs 16:32).

GROWTH

After more than eight years together in one united ministry, Hoskins Park Ministries grew to a staff of eight, a staff we felt God called for the sake of the same discipleship Johnny and I had experienced, one that was not hired because of their resumes, but because the Lord led them to us, with all their baggage, for His glory. One came right out of jail on a mentorship program sponsored by the state. Hoskins Park helps broken people who need a second chance. And He uses leaders as His instruments to help them find it. Hoskins Park doesn't fire someone because they want him or her to be more productive.

It was our intent to enter into discipleship relationships, realizing that the people we hired or worked with may be one of our twelve disciples rather than part of our business; it was similar to marriage but without the divorce part. And it's hard to fire a calling! *No other model worked for us.* It was a great experience. Until my experience with Johnny, I had not understood it.

A SUBTLE MISS

While Johnny and I were being taught this version of discipleship, I was struggling with the local church over the same issue, except it was about me. If Johnny truly was a version of Private Ryan in my life then I was a version of Captain Miller in his life, the officer sent to rescue Private Ryan. I needed the rest of the Second Ranger Battalion around me, too. But because of the fragmentation of our Christian army, something I address in later chapters, I was without those other soldiers. And a lone captain won't last long in a war trying to save a private. That is how I felt. There was no army with me—at least not one experienced with the circumstances I was facing.

HELP

I had never been in a war, but I felt like I was in one when I moved into Hoskins. For a period of time I heard gunshots in the vicinity of my house just about every night. Each time I did, I found myself physically shaking as I got down on my knees in the middle of the night to pray. My neighbor across the street was stabbed, and another fellow was shot and killed next door. Additionally, I was trying to adjust to the culture of Hoskins Park, a culture that was often in total contradiction to my own, one in which paying taxes, keeping records, having enforceable boundaries, respecting authority, staying calm in the midst of arguments were all optional and subjective to the individual: these were all factors of poverty, according to Dr. Payne.

That is why *I* needed help.

MY NEED FOR DISCIPLESHIP

I needed people who had the time to walk with me, listen to me, understand this battle, and help me on this journey into Satan's stomping grounds. Or tell me to get out. While God healed me of many of my past wounds, I was still just a man, and the enemy doesn't flee never to return. He just waits until the right time to attack—again. I knew that time was nearing as I continued to be worn down with a standing army that appeared to be clueless to the dangers that threatened me. It's one thing to think you are a soldier in a war; it's quite another to actually be one. I had a few close friends that God used to keep me sane during the initial days, but I still needed people who understood what I was dealing with, who could help me do this work the right way. *I needed to be mentored by a mature Christian leader who was experienced in poverty.* The members of my former church didn't have any experience with poverty, and the leaders who did, didn't have the time. Support did come, though. Many generous people volunteered to help us work on the property, fix up our houses on Saturdays, participate in a special project or donate money to help us go forward. And the senior pastor of my home church, one of my greatest supporters, included me in a group of very successful businessmen who purchased three houses in the Hoskins area.

As generous as people were, including my cherished church, we still needed that battalion of soldiers, experienced generals and proper funding to impact this war on poverty. Funding the expansion of organizations like Hoskins Park is often easier than funding the operations of the ministry; overhead has been given a bad rap because of past abuses. But without overhead, there are no people or resources to manage the ministry efficiently. A Catch-22. You need both. And part-time and busy volunteers cannot appropriately fill the holes. Right or wrong, I still believed the spiritual support and the money to hire the dedicated and called folks we needed to mature should come from the body of Christ, the local church. Without the local church partnering with Hoskins to a greater degree than they were, another entity had to fill the gap. The only group I felt could and should take that role was the board of directors. But getting and sustaining a healthy board strong enough to fill this role had its own challenges. On top of that, after fifteen years, I was exhausted.

CHAPTER 7
QUESTIONS

1. What is your definition of a "disciple"?

2. How much interaction do you feel should take place in the discipleship process? Do you think the one being discipled and his or her mentor should meet once a week, once a month, or more or less often than that?

3. What might prevent meeting to the degree you think is necessary for a quality discipleship relationship?

4. Do you have the time for that?

8 A Strong Board to "Fill the Gap"

"Most people go to the cross but never get on the cross."
—Leonard Ravenhill

THE BOARD

The IRS typically requires at least three distinct board members for any 501(c)(3) nonprofit organization. Besides this government requirement, there are legal, ethical, and practical reasons for a board: the board is the gatekeeper for the organization. It should ensure supporters that the organization is governed appropriately. If there is not a supportive board of directors in a nonprofit you support, you are likely enabling that organization to exist without proper boundaries.

For most of the years I was with Hoskins Park, I was its executive director and chairman of the board. In the beginning of the life cycle of an organization, having the same person holding those two positions is normal. But as an organization matures, it can be an obstacle to growth, either because of the leader's limitations or other factors they cannot control. The fact that I was in both of these roles was a blessing and a curse for me and for Hoskins Park. The blessing was that people trusted me to do what I said. They did not worry about their money being misused or how Hoskins Park was being managed. The curse was that everyone expected me to do everything—all by myself. If I suggested to the board that they needed to be more engaged and provide financial stability for the ministry, I was either rebuked or regarded strangely.

MY MISUNDERSTANDING—NOT THEIRS

To be fair, I never thought the board would have to be as important as they became. I expected the board to support my efforts to develop the ministry, involve their churches in our work, be a cheerleader for the ministry, encourage me spiritually, and help us be accountable to what we said we were doing and to what we should be doing. Those are actually reasonable expectations. I also expected an evolutionary process for the board and its members with a

59

greater focus on funding as the ministry matured. But when the parachurch model intersected with the local church while I was being blindsided by the issues inherent in dealing with those in poverty, the board needed to step up. That meant having people who could understand something that was too complicated for them to understand without having experienced it themselves. I was left wondering what I should do.

IDEAS

Since I was handling the operations of the ministry, meaning everything outside of the internal day-to-day management of the facility, when the financial pressures were on, I did not have time to constantly explain the challenge of this work to the board—although I tried. I would encourage new board members to get involved when some of the existing board members could not help any further, but they came up with great, but already tried, ideas. Without proper training and experience most middle-class people just cannot understand the issues we were discussing, whether they are serving on an urban board or not.

What I needed was their personal financial support and their time—the two things most could not give to any great extent. It was not fair to them in many ways. They thought typical business ideas could and would work and wanted to implement these proven ideas—but they would not work with our environment. We tried starting a thrift shop and lawn service, we had fund raising campaigns, we used social media outlets, and we sponsored a local race for the poor called OneStep. I even wrote my first book, *Second Wind*, for the sake of funding. But all of these required more resources than we had in order to generate sufficient return. They also distracted me from my own call to be a pastor. Trying to explain that proved impossible. And once you get behind the eight ball, things become pressurized, and we were behind the eight ball. People felt the pressure from me, which became an obstacle to support. I also tried to recruit folks to the board who were already involved in Hoskins Park but who were comfortable keeping their distance. It was the same gap I found when I started a secular organization: one between those with means and those who had a passion to change the world. We just couldn't offer the promise of financial gains with our work, so the worldly incentive to commit was much reduced. Of course the eternal incentive should be there—but because of the issues I will discuss, most folks living comfortably in the United States do not have that level of faith.

Only recently did I read Payne's *Bridges Out of Poverty*. From now on, it will be required reading for anyone I am trying to help who wants to engage with the poor unless they complete a training program before helping. We cannot let people get on our board of directors who are not trained in the essentials of the poverty culture. It just doesn't work. Those involved with the poor must have core competencies to engage in this work, or else they might undermine the work in their efforts to help. And they need to be mature Christians—on fire for Christ—real soldiers. The ones normally found on staff at the local church.

BOARD CHAIR

I turned the board chair position over to a competent board member in order to encourage additional support and leadership. He inherited the board as it was but started "leading" them, something I was unable to do as effectively as he was. Maybe that was because they knew he had a full-time job but was still committed to helping at a higher level. Regardless, he gave out assignments and held folks accountable for results. He was being a leader and he engaged financially. Things were progressing quite well and I felt the relief I had always been praying for. Then something happened on the Hoskins Park leadership team that caught me off-guard: two of our staff members engaged in behavior unbecoming of followers of Christ. While things like this happen from time to time in most organizations, I felt convicted that I had been overlooking the personal accountability of our leadership team for "business" results—the very thing I stood against. When I tried to explain my convictions to Johnny and the board, offering an immediate response to downsize the ministry, it was met with resistance. Johnny and I butted heads like we had done years ago. There have been two times in the history of the ministry when the board of directors really understood what was going on in the ministry and when the Hoskins staff truly understood the issues we faced. In both cases it was when I left. The first time I needed a sabbatical before I got married. This was the second time. I was simply doing what I thought necessary to ensure Hoskins' survival and my own spiritual health: get out of the way at the expense of my job and allow Hoskins to reorganize to a more manageable size with more people engaged to help and give me time to catch my second wind. Since I have always known this was God's ministry, it was not that difficult to stand aside.

Unlike many people who have started organizations, I did not start Hoskins Park because I wanted to start another organization. I knew how hard successful organizations are to begin and manage through my secular experience. *I had been put in a position that resulted in Hoskins Park.* Once put in that position, however, I had done my job instinctively. I did all I could to ensure Hoskins Park's success as I truly believed I had joined God in His work with the poor. I still believe that to be true. We grew to be the third-largest ministry in Charlotte sheltering homeless men. But something wasn't quite right. Maybe it was me. Or maybe it was something else.

NOW WHAT?
I had to let Hoskins go. Before I could make another move, I had to understand exactly what was going on:

How did I get here?
Where am I?
What do I do now?

That led me to analyze Hoskins Park and look at it from angles I might have missed before. I call these my AHA moments. Discussing these is our next topic.

"A sum can be put right: but only by going back till you find the error and working it afresh from that point, never by simply going on."
—C.S. Lewis, *The Great Divorce*

CHAPTER 8
QUESTIONS

1. What is the role of the board of directors in a nonprofit?

2. What do you think the role of the board should be (if different)?

3. If you are on a board or considering one, do you think you have a fiscal responsibility to support the funding of the mission and the vision of the organization? If so, to what extent? If not, who do you think should be responsible for funding?

4. What experience do you think a board member should have to be on a board?

5. If you are on a nonprofit board right now and if it were changed to be a for-profit business, what would you do differently than you are currently doing as a board member—particularly if all of your money was invested in the organization?

6. Based upon your answer, what is preventing you from making those changes?

PART TWO

MY AHA MOMENTS

WHAT EVERY CHRISTIAN SHOULD CONSIDER BEFORE ENGAGING THE POOR

9 Unrealistic Expectations and a Wrong Definition of Success

"The punch that knocks you out is the one you didn't see."
—Joe Frazier

AHA MOMENTS

There were five major issues that caught me off guard in my work with the poor. I call them my AHA moments. They are:

1. Unrealistic expectations for those I wanted to help.
2. Misunderstanding the parachurch model that I was part of.
3. Fragmentation of the Christian Army over money.
4. Discovery of the mysterious, but real, Christian industry.
5. A shallow and busy discipleship process in our local churches that hampered our effectiveness.

The first AHA moment was my own unrealistic expectations for helping the homeless. It is similar to a parent who births what appears to be a healthy child but over time discovers that child has a disability. There is nothing wrong with a disability—but without everyone knowing what the disability is, life is much harder for all of those involved, particularly the one with the disability and his or her caretaker. This AHA moment was discovering my kid(s), the participants at Hoskins Park, were disabled.

THE HOMELESS

Hoskins Park Ministries takes care of some of the most critical of the homeless population—not just physically but mentally. They don't always look like the stereotypical homeless person, but they are very lost souls. They typically have minimal education, felony records, deeply addictive behaviors, broken relationships, distrustful attitudes, and a lot of difficulty understanding boundaries. Most of them come from generational poverty. After years of trying to help, I realized I had greatly underestimated how difficult the lives of the homeless have become and how difficult it was to help someone who had gone through so much hell in life.

From a personal standpoint, the diagram that follows illustrates my misunderstanding. The first continuum was what I thought when I first moved into the urban part of Charlotte. Regardless of their condition, I believed our participants were able to get and hold a job, restore relationships, get connected with a local church, live on their own, and live a healthier life free from the addiction that once controlled them. I figured that would happen over a one- to five-year period of time.

Continuum of Care in 2002

A — Average timeframe 1-5 years — Z

This is the continuum of care I THOUGHT I was going to provide for those without a home when I started back in 2002 at Hoskins Park Ministries.

• Addiction to a substance	• Free from addiction	• Employed	• Budgeting their money	• Restored relationships	• Steady job	• Law abiding citizen
• Unloved - non-Christian values		• Have found a Church home	• Tithing	• Respectful and appreciative attitude		• Church home/family
• Criminal background						• On a workable budget
• Issues that have developed over the years						• Restored relationships
• Disrespectful						• Living on own w/own place
						• Living a healthier life (physically)

REALITY

The second continuum is what I found to be more realistic. The majority of them were not going to be living on their own, or going to their own church, or working a steady job, or restoring broken relationships, or maintaining a budget and living a healthier life after five years. They were going to be making better choices, understanding their choices had consequences, obeying the law, and many will have given up the addiction that put them or kept them on the street. That is a far different person than I originally thought when I moved into the Hoskins area. I misunderstood the impact that a broken family had on a person. I have since discovered that the destruction of the traditional family may be one of the main factors contributing to the homeless population. It begins the cycle of poverty. Then there is the lack of education that typically accompanies broken families and those in poverty. I don't consider education the key to success like many do, but a lack of a good education puts a person, any person, at a disadvantage. It is also something folks, including Martin Luther King Jr., believed was essential to the development of the African-American community. A poor education, combined with a negative self-worth because most of the homeless are typically raised without a dad, meant the recovery time necessary for our residents was substantially more than I had thought. You don't lose 200 pounds overnight. And you don't rehabilitate someone who has been through a train wreck overnight, either.

UNREALISTIC EXPECTATIONS

Most people, just like me, have no idea how generational poverty impacts the homeless, so they have unrealistic expectations for their progress, particularly for those who are mentally ill and look good on the outside but are in torment on the inside. They think that if they were given some relief, they could thrive. That is not always true. Even after our objections, someone bought $300 worth of tools for a participant of Hoskins Park Ministries. The participant immediately sold those tools and used the money for drugs. He ended up back on the streets. Most of us are ill-equipped to deal with folks who do not look like us. Anyone who is not experienced or trained in poverty will not understand the culture they are dealing with and therefore will likely try to do the right thing—the wrong way. That is who I used to be.

Can an average American, living as one of the richest people in the world, understand how to help someone in poverty? I have come to believe the answer is no, not without proper training and/or experience.

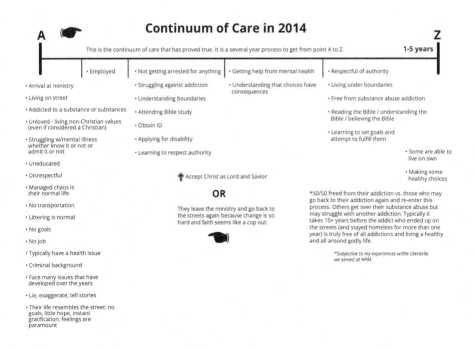

Continuum of Care in 2014

A   Z

This is the continuum of care that has proved true. It is a several year process to get from point A to Z.   **1-5 years**

| | • Employed | • Not getting arrested for anything | • Getting help from mental health | • Respectful of authority |

• Arrival at ministry

• Living on street

• Addicted to a substance or substances

• Unloved - living non-Christian values (even if considered a Christian)

• Struggling w/mental illness whether know it or not or admit it or not

• Uneducated

• Disrespectful

• Managed chaos is their normal life

• No transportation

• Littering is normal

• No goals

• No job

• Typically have a health issue

• Criminal background

• Face many issues that have developed over the years

• Lie, exaggerate, tell stories

• Their life resembles the street: no goals, little hope, instant gratification, feelings are paramount

• Struggling against addiction

• Understanding boundaries

• Attending Bible study

• Obtain ID

• Applying for disability

• Learning to respect authority

✝ Accept Christ as Lord and Savior

OR

They leave the ministry and go back to the streets again because change is so hard and faith seems like a cop out.

• Understanding that choices have consequences

• Living under boundaries

• Free from substance abuse addiction

• Reading the Bible / understanding the Bible / believing the Bible

• Learning to set goals and attempt to fulfill them

• Some able to live on own

• Making some healthy choices

*50/50 freed from their addiction vs. those who may go back to their addiction again and re-enter this process. Others get over their substance abuse but may struggle with another addiction. Typically it takes 10+ years before the addict who ended up on the streets (and stayed homeless for more than one year) is truly free of all addictions and living a healthy and all around godly life.

*Subjective to my experiences w/the clientele we served at HPM.

ONE IN CHRIST

Dr. Ruby Payne agrees. She explains in *Bridges Out of Poverty* that helping the poor is much more complicated than most of us realize. One of the reasons for that is the distinction of classes. I know, as Christians we are supposed to be one in Christ:

> There is neither Jew nor Gentile, neither slave nor free, nor is there male and female, for you are all one in Christ Jesus (Galatians 3:28).

But that is not always the case. Our focus on race, class, gender, level of poverty, etc., is often worldly and judgmental. The truth is we don't always accept one another as "one in Christ" despite God's desire that we would and should. Maybe that is because we don't understand one another. Explanations like the one that follow are an attempt to help us understand our differences so that we can be "one" in body. Therefore it is relevant to our discussion.

CLASS DIFFERENCES ARE REAL

Dr. Payne defines the differences in people using three classes:

1. Those in poverty,
2. The middle class, and
3. The wealthy.

Rather than sticking to traditional barriers that separate classes, especially money, she differentiates the classes using several categories. Here is an excerpt from *Bridges Out of Poverty*:[20]

Financial: Having the money to purchase goods and services.

Emotional: Being able to choose and control emotional responses, particularly to negative situations, without engaging in self-destructive behavior. This is an internal resource and shows itself through stamina, perseverance, and choices.

Mental: Having the mental abilities and acquired skills (reading, writing, computing) to deal with daily life.

Spiritual: Believing in divine purpose and guidance.

Physical: Having physical health and mobility.

Support Systems: Having friends, family, and backup resources available to access in times of need. These are external resources.

Relationships/Role Models: Having frequent access to adult(s) who are appropriate, who are *nurturing* to the child, and who do not engage in self-destructive behavior.

20. Ibid. 11.

Knowledge of Hidden Rules: Knowing the unspoken cues and habits of a group.

Coping Strategies: Being able to engage in procedural self-talk and the mindsets that allow issues to be moved from the concrete to the abstract. It is the ability to translate from the personal to the issue.

The degree to which a person *does without these resources* is the degree to which they find themselves in *poverty*. The folks Hoskins Park Ministries cares for are typically without these resources. Take another look at the list. Notice only one of those topics is financial.

Dr. Payne includes a list of questions in her book that allow individuals to assess their "class." I recommend you read her book. In the meantime you can take a shot at knowing your class by taking my shorter quiz of these questions listed below:

1. *Do you have a bucket list?* If yes, you are not living in a culture of poverty.
2. *Was a formal education inhibited by your life's circumstances and therefore something you were unable to achieve beyond high school?* If yes, you are more likely to be part of a culture of poverty.
3. *When the police approach, are you more grateful or fearful?* For the most part, if you are not fearful, you are likely not living in poverty.
4. *Is or was a college education an assumed expectation in your life or for the life of your children?* If yes, you are likely classified as middle class or wealthy.

Still wonder? Consider the information that follows as further clarification, starting with this information from the Credit Suisse report:

Someone who has US $3,650, which includes equity in a home, is among the wealthiest half of the population of the world. If someone has US $77,000 they are in the top 10% of global wealth holders, and for those with upwards of $798,000, they are in the top 1%.[21]

Now you can assess yourself based upon their information. Do you have $3,650 in your car, home, assets, or in the bank? If so, you are among the top 50% of the wealthiest people in the world. Do you have $77,000 in equity, assets, in your retirement account, or in the bank? If so, you are in the top 10% of the richest people in the world. Does your family of three live on less

---

21. Treanor, Jill. "Richest 1% of People Own Nearly Half of Global Wealth, Says Report." The Guardian. October 15, 2014. Accessed October 1, 2015.

than $19,000 annually, or your family of four on less than $25,000? Then you live in poverty.[22]

DIFFERENCES

Money is the obvious factor differentiating those in poverty and those who have resources. And, while that is typically true, other aspects of poverty were eye-openers for me. For instance, those in poverty are much more prepared to physically fight when they are pushed than those of another class since that behavior was more prevalent in their family and life. The wealthy tend to alienate or ignore those who offend them. The middle class are somewhere in the middle ground between a physical confrontation and total alienation. Spiritually the poor tend to be fatalistic, life is predetermined, while the middle class considers their efforts to be significant in determining their fate. They have a tendency to believe that what happens in life is up to one's efforts. It is middle-class people who think the Bible says, "God helps those who help themselves," when the Bible does not say that at all. In point of fact, it was Benjamin Franklin who made that saying popular. The wealthy have trouble believing in spiritual matters since they are relatively self-sufficient, at least in their minds. Religion threatens their wealth if they don't redefine it to suit their lifestyle. Remember the rich man in the Bible? He believed he was doing everything correctly, but would not part from his money when Jesus asked him to "give it up."

Classes are further defined by uncovering hidden rules or definitions over the following terms:

Possessions, money, personality, social emphasis, food, clothing, time, education, destiny, language, family structure, worldview, love, driving forces, and humor.[23]

What that means is that each class views each of these areas differently, thus creating communication barriers that are not evident to those involved. When cultures clash over something like perceived excessive use of force by law enforcement, few understand how to help because the classes are unable to communicate. This is why personal relationships are so important when we want to help others, particularly those of another class. *We have to understand what they are hearing when we speak and they have to understand what*

22. http://www.dollarsandsense.org/archives/2006/0106dollar.html. Accessed November 9, 2015. http://talkpoverty.org/basics/. Assessed November 10, 2015.
23. Payne, Ruby K., and Philip E. DeVol. *Bridges out of Poverty: Strategies for Professionals and Communities.* Revised ed. 11. 44-45.

we are saying when we speak. Otherwise everyone might as well be speaking a foreign language, which is pretty much how it is today for those untrained middle-class folks trying to help those in poverty.

THE LESSON

What I learned from this first AHA moment was the importance of working with people who are intimately involved and trained in dealing with the people we so desperately want to help. Those who have experienced poverty like Johnny, and *professionals who become immersed in the culture of poverty* and who have learned how to have proper expectations for those they help, are the ones who can make the best decisions and be truly effective.

If we are not working with those experienced, trained and immersed people, like it or not, we are wasting a lot of time and money. And that is true whether it is in America or another country. This is not just about the homeless. We may feel good about our help of those in need, but we may not be helping those who need the most help—those in the trenches, those on the front lines. As Jen Hatmaker writes in her book, *For the Love: Fighting for Grace in a World of Impossible Standards*:

> "As uneducated, inexperienced outsiders, we must work with people who live and work and breathe the sustainable, holistic health of their community. We need trusted experts here. These trips are too costly—in human and financial capital—to fly halfway around the world to put on a puppet show. High-capacity local leaders who are capable of affecting long-term benefits to their communities are essential. We should be floored by their aptitude and awed by their vision for development, which will include short- and long-term goals, measurable outcomes, and educated solutions."[24]

This leads me to the second AHA moment—the fragmentation of our Christian army. A great part of our Christian army is trying to win a war without being totally committed. We should support the most committed Christians around us whether they are in the local church or a parachurch organization.

---

24. Hatmaker, Jen. *For the Love: Fighting for Grace in a World of Impossible Standards.* Nashville, Tenn.: Nelson Books, 2015. 158.

CHAPTER 9
QUESTIONS

1. What assumptions have you made in your life that proved to be incorrect or that somehow hurt you?

2. How well do you understand the challenges of someone in poverty?

3. Have you overcome an addiction? Do you know someone who has successfully overcome a serious addiction? How might that impact your ability to help addicts?

4. What crisis have you faced in your own life that has made you more understanding about those in the same crisis?

5. When you are faced with a crisis that requires professional help, will anyone do? What selection process have you used to select a professional to help you out of a difficult situation? Does their training matter? Does their experience matter? Why or why not?

10 The Fragmentation of the Christian Army Through the Parachurch Model

"Problems are not stop signs, they are guidelines."
—Robert H. Schuller

THE MYSTERIOUS PARACHURCH

The second AHA moment was my misunderstanding of the parachurch or nonprofit model. From an "industry" standpoint and unbeknownst to me when I started, Hoskins Park Ministries is categorized as a parachurch. This is where my train *derailed* from its tracks for the second time. Here is the definition of a parachurch:

> A Christian faith-based organization that works outside of and across denominations to engage in social welfare and evangelism, usually independent of church oversight. These bodies can be businesses, non-profit corporations, or private associations.[25]

That means a parachurch is independent from the local church. Call me naive but I had come to believe that God intended to change the world *through* the local church, so why would I ever want to leave that body and why would they want to leave me? That does not mean I don't like the model; the model can work. What I don't like is that *the model fragments the Christian army* if the local church and parachurches are not in partnership—and they are not, at least to the degree I am suggesting. I have found there are three primary reasons why the church has difficulty partnering with the typical parachurch organization and three reasons why the parachurch has difficulty partnering with the local church. I must add a caveat here that I am not referring to the minority of well-established and mature parachurch organizations such as the Salvation Army, an organization that has its own army and congregation, and has remained Christ-centered. I am referring to the vast number of smaller organizations trying to mature or those that have matured by dismissing their Christian values.

---

25. "Parachurch Organization." Wikipedia Dictionary. Accessed September 30, 2015.

Let's start with the problems the church has with many parachurch organizations:

1. The issue of funding.
2. The issue of productivity.
3. The issue of leadership competency.

FUNDING

One reason the churches don't want to be too strictly tied to parachurch organizations is because supporters of the mission of the parachurch might believe all the funding needs to come from that church and ignore the fact that the church has a budget beyond the "parachurch's mission." A potential partnering church wants other churches to get involved in the financial support of these organizations so they don't "own them." It is too big of a financial commitment and burden on a typical church. One local pastor shared his experience when the parachurch he started was affiliated with his own church. He said none of the neighboring churches would support the parachurch as long as there was such a connection. He chose to reduce the affiliation for the purpose of encouraging more local church support, and it worked. Since then, however, the founding church stopped supporting the parachurch because it is no longer comfortable about how the organization is being managed. It set the organization free but in its freedom the parachurch became less accountable to the Christian values set by the church. I deal with this in the next AHA moment, but consider the question as we move forward: was it the right decision to set the parachurch free over money?

Another issue with funding regards the leaders of the parachurch organization itself. If a parachurch leadership team believes one church is responsible for all of their funding, they might become sloppy or irresponsible with their program. When I started my first company, having worked for Apple Computer for several years, I used a piece of letterhead to write a note to my partner. When he got the note he quickly let me know we were not Apple Computer and it was inappropriate for me to use letterhead, costing a cent or two, instead of scrap paper, which costs nothing. I got it. Parachurch leaders must understand the value of a dollar, and they may not if a church fully funds them.

PRODUCTIVITY

Another reason the two don't typically partner is because of the issue of productivity. Churches believe in the mission and work of the parachurch organization they support, but many have a broader mission and mandate: evangelism and discipleship of the masses and help for the global poor. While they support the work of a particular parachurch organization, the church wants to do more than that, and many can. Or they are self-focused. They have no hard feelings about these independent organizations; they just need them to stay independent so they can stay focused on their own mission.

UNCOOPERATIVE LEADERS

Finally, the church finds many parachurch leaders uncooperative and difficult to deal with. The typical grass-roots leader is streetwise, having experienced the same issues as the people they are trying to help, but sometimes incapable of running an efficient and legal organization: something most churches rightly demand. *The Profit* is a television show about a business professional named Marcus Lemonis who comes alongside struggling people to help rescue their businesses from failure. Besides sound business advice, he invests thousands of dollars to make these businesses profitable. The show once featured an organization called Tonnie's Minis, a failing do-it-yourself cupcake bakery owned by Tonnie Razier in Manhattan. His wife, Erenisse, had invested approximately $250,000 in the business and did not think the business would make it without help, so she called Marcus. The first thing Marcus did was assess costs to find the problems in the business. He asked Tonnie, a great salesman but not-so-good manager, how much it cost to make one cupcake. Tonnie did not have an exact number. Marcus added up the actual costs and found they were much higher than Tonnie's estimates, which was part of the reason the organization was failing. Tonnie didn't believe that his inability to accurately count costs was the cause of their problems. In fact, he was ready to open another location: he thought he just had to sell more. Marcus disagreed with his strategy and they bumped heads. Finally Marcus and Erenisse forced Tonnie to reveal more information regarding his business including all his expenses and debts. This is what they found: he had private loans from friends and family, tax bills, outstanding back pay to employees, and most shocking of all, a debt to a loan shark. Couple this with the fact that Tonnie was completely unaware of how all his debt in addition to his operating expenses and the cost of raw materials figured into the cost of one little cupcake, and you had a situation that looked impossible to solve.

The situation was precarious for one major reason: Tonnie was unable to see his own shortcomings—or admit them. Until Tonnie swallowed his pride and starting listening to Marcus and doing what he said, things did not change.[26] Tonnie finally listened and the business started to turn around.

POLIS STUDY IN CENTRAL FLORIDA

An assessment done by The Polis Institute in Central Florida found this to be true in their own work with nonprofits (parachurches):

> "Nonprofit leaders often have the passion and experience to provide services to the marginalized people of our city. However, many nonprofits are challenged operationally with running an organization and lack the resources necessary to stay on the front lines of the work. They lacked business or administrative skills that allowed for a greater chance of success of the organization."[27]

PROPER ORGANIZATION

My experience suggests that the leaders do not know how to put fair, proper and enforceable boundaries on their work. They consider the only boundaries worth having are the ones the leader chooses based on their feelings. As a result, some of these same parachurch leaders don't know they are incapable of running a maturing organization since they cannot understand that boundaries cannot be subject to their feelings. Their calling is often considered God-given; therefore, no one can instruct them in typical business structures. While these leaders are passionate about their work, many in the church find their passion close to arrogance as they often want what they want when they want it. Anyone who gets in their way becomes their apparent enemy. This is not perceived as healthy by the church, nor deserving of their support. Therefore, the issue for the church is whether someone has the time to disciple these messy and passionate leaders. Sometimes they do not because it is not consistent with their definition of success. They are focused on production, not discipleship. They should find someone somewhere to step in but typically do not.

PROBLEMS WITH THE LOCAL CHURCH

On the other hand there are three primary reasons parachurch leaders have difficulty with the local church. They are:

---

26. Duffy, Paula. "THE PROFIT Recap: Marcus Rescued Tonnie's Minis From Owner's Wishful Thinking." TVRuckus. May 25, 2015. Accessed October 1, 2015.

27. Seneff, Jim. "Seeking the Welfare of the City: An Assessment from a Christian Perspective of How Human Needs Are Met in Central Florida." Polis Institute. November 14, 2009. Accessed October 1, 2015.

1. The issue of control.
2. The issue of urgency.
3. The issue of funding.

CONTROLLING CHURCH

First, parachurch leaders don't want the church to control their work, and they have their reasons. As the Polis Institute discovered:

"Church partnerships can be helpful but also hindering because of the desired level of control and the lack of commitment (by the church)."[28]

They don't believe church leaders have the experience to help them in their program. They don't think they can relate to the struggle of the poor they are trying to help. Most church leaders have never lived in "the hood" or in a poor area, nor do they typically understand the differences between the poor and middle class. Therefore, parachurch leaders don't think church leaders can relate to their work because, well, they can't.

Again, from the Polis Institute:

"The church is called to social and spiritual renewal of the city, yet many churches are either immobile or conduct high-profile relief efforts that do not result in transformation. Community development experts would argue that these efforts may be damaging in that they foster dependencies and unhealthy perceptions of inferiority and superiority. Resource-rich churches often try to impose a vision from outside a distressed neighborhood and do not work to understand the hopes, concerns, and assets of the residents in the neighborhood. The majority of the churches within the distressed neighborhoods are focused either strictly on word-of-mouth evangelism or serving parishioners outside the neighborhood."[29]

Parachurches are independent from the local church because parachurch leaders don't think the church knows enough to hold them accountable for reasonable results. The results to which the church wants to hold the para-church accountable are not accurate or reasonable. This is very similar to the way I expected particular change in a person within five years at Hoskins. I did not understand the real issues, and many times neither does the church.

---

28. Ibid.
29. Ibid.

TOO BUREAUCRATIC

Second, their belief is that the local church is too bureaucratic and therefore takes too much time to get things done. This is particularly true of smaller and less-mature parachurch organizations. Many of these new organizations are dealing with people in crisis that they believe cannot always "wait until tomorrow" when that is just what the church wants them to do: wait. But they won't wait. This issue is about response time. Parachurch organizations are independent because the urgency of their work is more reflective of the emergency room of a hospital. And that is too demanding for the structures and bureaucracy of the local church that often acts more like the general hospital.

MONEY

Finally, most parachurch leaders feel the tithe the church receives to do the work they do is unfairly distributed. Parachurch leaders need funds and are forced to go find them outside the local church. This can create a feeling of division, animosity, and competition or it can "burn out" a parachurch leader as he or she seeks additional employment outside of their parachurch work. Sadly, it may also be the single biggest factor dividing our army. Because of its importance it became my third AHA moment.

CHAPTER 10
QUESTIONS

1. Were you aware that Christian nonprofits are called parachurch organizations?

2. What did you learn about the issue between the church and parachurch?

3. Do you understand the problem?

4. How can you help?

11 The Greatest Issue Fragmenting Our Army: Money

"Americanized Christians often fight to make sure our taxes are lower, fight to repeal health care for poor people, and throw a fit over a small portion of our income going to provide food stamps. While touting 'voluntary' and 'private' charity as the way to go, we give on average 2%-3% of our income to the church or charities—not nearly enough to actually address the needy in any meaningful way."[30]

The third AHA moment was the unfortunate recognition that money is the biggest factor fragmenting the Christian Army.

I want to state in advance that as the reader, you will need to pay particular attention to the bridge I build in this chapter to an upcoming AHA moment: the true cost and definition of discipleship. There is no way to solidify the point about money without a discussion about discipleship. A casual read may leave you somewhere on the bridge without any ability to cross it. Let's get started with a discussion of the tithe and the model of church we find in the book of Acts.

TEN PERCENT

The Hebrew and Greek definition of tithe is "tenth." Tithing is the practice of "tenthing" from our income:[31] giving God 10 percent of one's income. It is found several times in the Bible, but first when Abram vows a tenth to Melchizedek, king of Salem and priest of God Most High (Genesis 14:20). Subsequently it is found in Genesis (28:20-22) in the story of Jacob and then in other places such as Leviticus 27:32, Deuteronomy 14:22, Nehemiah 10:38 and Hebrews 7:5. Most understand the tithe as 10% of our gross or net income and most church leaders believe the tithe should go to the local church. In fact, that is what I taught when I was on staff at my church, not

---

30. Ibid.
31. Kelly, Russell Earl. "The Origin and Definition of Tithing." Should the Church Teach Tithing? A Theologian's Rebuttal of a Taboo Doctrine. February 2007. Accessed September 30, 2015.

because I thought the nonprofits (parachurches) doing God's work should not be properly funded, but my expectation was that the local church properly funded the ministries it felt called to support. My reference point for this model is found in the book of Acts:

> They devoted themselves to the apostles' teaching and to fellowship, to the breaking of bread and to prayer. Everyone was filled with awe at the many wonders and signs performed by the apostles. All the believers were together and had everything in common. They sold property and possessions to give to anyone who had need. Every day they continued to meet together in the temple courts. They broke bread in their homes and ate together with glad and sincere hearts, praising God and enjoying the favor of all the people. And the Lord added to their number daily those who were being saved (Acts 2:42-47).

TRUE COMMUNITY

These believers "were together," and "had everything in common"; they met every day and "sold property and possessions" to give to anyone who had a need. That is intimate community. It implies that they knew the needs of the people in their church. One cannot fill a need one is not aware of. When the needs of those in the church are known and met, it would follow that *if they had created a parachurch to support those members the needs of the parachurch would also have been met.* They would designate certain people to fulfill the areas that many parachurch organizations were founded to fill today. Thus my assumption that the parachurches that my church supported were well-funded. Consider this example from the early church when believers discovered unmet needs in the church:

> In those days when the number of disciples was increasing, the Hellenistic Jews among them complained against the Hebraic Jews because their widows were being overlooked in the daily distribution of food. So the Twelve gathered all the disciples together and said, "It would not be right for us to neglect the ministry of the word of God in order to wait on tables. Brothers and sisters, choose seven men from among you who are known to be full of the Spirit and wisdom. We will turn this responsibility over to them and will give our attention to prayer and the ministry of the word." This proposal pleased the whole group. They chose Stephen, a man full of faith and

of the Holy Spirit; also Philip, Procorus, Nicanor, Timon, Parmenas, and Nicolas from Antioch, a convert to Judaism (Acts 6:1-5).

They did not start an independent organization to feed widows. Instead they figured out a way to allocate the proper food for them among their group, the church. *But had they started a parachurch back then*, the funds to support "the need" would have come from the alms of local believers that understood the need and knew it was their responsibility to satisfy it. In other words those funds would have come from the tithe given to the local church.

TODAY

Today things are different. Because of technology and the increased size of many of our churches, we are now aware and able to help people all around the world. This is the positive side of larger congregations and our advances in technology. The church gets news about starving children in Third World countries or worldwide tragedies and sends money to help. All good. The negative side is that we get so busy meeting worldwide needs, and using money as the panacea, that we forget our own call to our family. That means we miss the needy folks in our own cities—people who are often being cared for by a parachurch organization. These parachurch organizations were created to focus on the specific needs of the local community just like the disciples were chosen to feed widows in the first-century church. They should be properly funded by the tithe.

THE BRIDGE WE NEED TO CROSS

The tithe, collected by the local church, is supposed to be used to support the special needs of the community, but it runs dry because it now supports these worldwide needs. That is how an organization like Hoskins Park, a ministry that cares for homeless men, can be overlooked when it comes to the tithe. Of course an argument could be made for continued support of Third World countries and tragedies we hear about on the news. They need help. But money is not the only help we should give; it is only one aspect of the cure. This brings us to the bridge I mentioned in the beginning and presents two issues: Because we do not always have strong relationships with the people or places we send our money, much of it gets wasted. That is the first issue. We don't really know whom we are dealing with or whether we can trust them to do what they say they are going to do with our money. Technology has allowed those in the West to have large numbers of surface-level friendships, which results in a lukewarm level of discipleship that is undermining our efforts to help transform cultures whether home or abroad. We are too busy to offer real answers to needs; we simply relieve them. But as one pastor recently declared, we may be feeding a lot of people who will go straight to hell if we don't start sharing the good news with them, which requires more of our time and a greater commitment on our part. It requires discipleship. And the discipleship to which I refer challenges a Westerner's idea of success. This brings us to the second issue.

THE LOSER

The focused parachurch organizations that are doing the work of the church are underfunded because, while they are part of the army, part of the body of Christ, they are without a proper share of the tithe because of all the aforementioned issues (i.e.: misunderstood expectations and issues that prevent the church and parachurch from a solid partnership). Thus they compete with the local church over money. The church might not see or care that this is competition because they have a stage and control their message. If I was ever asked to speak before a larger congregation when I was with Hoskins Park, I was typically told what message they wanted delivered and told to stick with that message. As a result, typical of all parachurch organizations, Hoskins had to develop its own "congregation" of supporters: normally folks who went to a church. Some call this the big "C" in the larger worldwide pool of Christians, considering the local church to be the little "c" in church, but the local church has the congregations and the stage in the local pool of Christians. It is the forum for Christians to hear and be taught the Word of God and therefore needs to be recognized as the generic church for purposes of my point.

DIVISION

Once supporters (the big "C" church) hear about our financial struggle, they too wonder why their (little "c") church is not more involved. I have looked at many of the local Christian nonprofits in Charlotte: most don't receive more than 10% of their budget from the local church. One *non-Christian organization* I looked at actually got more from the church than their Christian counterparts. Biblically, is that a functional model? I recall when my own financial support was ended when I left the local non-Christian shelter, which the church was supporting. Once the support is challenged then the parachurch has to seek other outlets for funding. One of those places is grants. But those "other sources" have their own built-in criteria that can distract the executive director from the real work at hand, helping those they want to help without becoming a fund-raiser.

GRANT

Years ago I was directed to a grant offered by a local organization desiring to help the homeless during the upcoming winter months. Because the grant was well-focused and had a time frame, winter, it appeared to be a perfect fit for Hoskins Park. Wanting to ensure the success of our proposal, I contacted their representative. Each time I discussed my proposal with the representative, he told me my application would likely be denied because it did not meet one of their less-important criteria. Therefore I had to rethink my application in order to secure funding. Finally after I was given another obstacle that appeared to be a Catch-22, I came right out and asked, "Do you want me to lie to get this grant?" That did not go over well at all, but that is the position I felt they were putting me in by their parameters. I submitted the grant, knowing the best way to help the homeless was to do exactly what I was proposing, but that required Hoskins Park to act before knowing whether we would get the grant or not: that was the Catch-22. It was the only way I could adhere to the grant's requirements without lying: start the work without the funding. Even though the grant was for winter, they announced the chosen organizations *in the spring.*

GRANTED

While I was grateful to be one of the organizations they decided to support, they gave us only one-third of the money we requested, one-third of what we needed to do the work. That meant the other two-thirds had to come from us, and we didn't have it. We struggled financially. When I was reviewing our numbers at the end of the year, I looked at how much we were short. It was the missing money from the grant. We did what we said, complied with the grant's parameters, took several more men off the streets during that cold winter, but because they did not fully fund the work, and didn't tell us until after the fact, it took us six months to financially recover. When details are misunderstood and funding is driven by those misunderstanding the details, not only is the Christian army fragmented, the entire model is shattered. And everyone is being steered by money. Are all of the folks applying for grants honest?

THEN WHAT HAPPENS?

The parachurch either remains under-resourced or starts to act more like a business. This may not be intentional; it's a result of their independence from the local church over time and their own struggle against numbers. The executive director of a parachurch becomes, most of all, a "fund raiser"—not a pastoral or spiritual leader. Remember the example from the previous AHA moment? The church set a parachurch free from their body in order to encourage funding from other churches. It worked. Other churches and organizations began to financially support them. But then the home church stopped financially supporting that same parachurch because the parachurch was not adhering to biblical standards that the church thought they should follow. Since the other organizations supporting the parachurch did not probe the issues that caused division with the mother church or even know about them, money was simply a tool to manufacture business results. The spiritual life of the leadership team was not even a consideration. But shouldn't the spiritual maturity of the leaders matter to everyone that supports a Christian organization?

PARACHURCHES ARE HELD ACCOUNTABLE TO BUSINESS RESULTS

Once funding is driving a maturing parachurch organization, they struggle to keep their Christian "C" intact. IRS-authorized 501(c)(3) nonprofits must have a board of directors to comply with the government's regulations as mentioned before, but that board is more often than not a formality for start-ups and used to ensure business results for a maturing organization. No matter where the organization is on the scale of maturity, most boards are governing boards (as opposed to hands-on managing boards) that hold the organization accountable to results that are not always in line with Christian principles and ideas or the appropriate definition of success. This approach allows a Christian organization to operate under non-Christian standards.

CHRISTIAN ORGANIZATIONS SHOULD BE DIFFERENT, BUT ARE THEY?

In partnership with the local church the parachurch can pursue its objectives without missing its Christian emphasis. The local church would hold it accountable as it should its own body. Without that partnership, because of the issue of funding and lack of accountability to the Bible, the parachurch is steered toward business results because businesspeople, not pastors, are often steering the ship. That does not mean there are not good people involved. It is simply not a sustainable model and may be one of the reasons the darkness continues to get darker: the Holy Spirit is no longer guiding our ship—we are. Discipleship is meant to transform lives; it takes a holistic approach. If that is sacrificed for our relief efforts, our model is broken. We must do both. And in order to do both we need more trained and committed soldiers led by the Holy Spirit of Jesus who are properly collaborating. But our Christian industry does not work that way, not yet anyway.

CHAPTER 11
QUESTIONS

1. What are your beliefs about "the tithe"?

2. Are you aware of the financial struggles of parachurches in your area?

3. Should parachurches operate like a business for the sake of "productivity"? Why or why not?

4. Why was Paul appealing to the Corinthians to give more? (See 2 Corinthians 8)

5. Is the parachurch organization you support accountable to any entity other than itself? If not, what are the internal measures taken by leadership to ensure leaders are accountable to biblical guidelines rather than business results?

12 The Unrecognized Christian Industry

"Every line is the perfect length if you don't measure it."
—Marty Rubin

The fourth AHA moment was understanding the mysterious but real industry that most of us are a part of as Christians. It is an industry without consistent or agreed-upon boundaries. Therefore it further fragments our Christian army. This is different from the aforementioned non-profit or parachurch model; this is the Protestant one.

To begin the discussion, consider these questions:

- Where and how does a church member discover his or her individual orders (calling)?

- What process does the church use to put non-staff people in their proper place as they mature during their journey?

- How do we assess our leaders in a biblical manner without crossing the line into a businesslike assessment process?

In order to explain this in the most understandable manner I need to use other industries that we are all aware of and understand. Consider teachers, coaches, and personal trainers, government employees addressing addictive behavior or poverty: all require certifications, if not degrees. There are built-in boundaries, assessments, and requirements to filter through all the opinions and well-intended people who think they can "fly jets" without proper training. While the "just do it" mentality has a place in the life of a Christian, it does not have a place without proper boundaries and assessment – at least not as it may require support. Let's take a look at the education and sports models.

EDUCATION

Children start kindergarten at five years old, and preschool at an even earlier age. If one goes through the entire process and earns a doctorate, one likely spends twenty-five years being educated.

Education Model

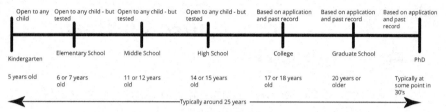

Report cards are given out throughout every student's educational career to assess their performance. The process is subject to the teacher and the assessment used and is important to ensure the person is developing properly. Standardized testing is also done at just about every grade level to evaluate proficiency. It is the basis by which we understand how well our student is learning in comparison to the others. A student cannot progress from stage to stage without proper performance.

ATHLETES

Sports are similar to the educational process. Let's use football as our example. A five- to fourteen-year-old child who wants to play football can start with the Peewee or Youth Football Leagues. At those levels, all a kid has to do is show up. High school football is next and requires a tryout. You don't make the team just because you show up on the field. The percentage of high school players that play college ball is less than 10%. It is hard to make the leap from high school to college. The percentage decreases for athletes to go from college to semi-pro or pro. You don't get to move into a more competitive environment if you don't prove yourself in your current environment. It's also not your choice.

Someone has to want you to play for their team. And you can't just start another team if the teams in the league do not choose you. If you want to play professional sports, you are going to do it the way it is set up in the league. You are also going to spend fourteen or more years training to get there. Like education, assessment matters.

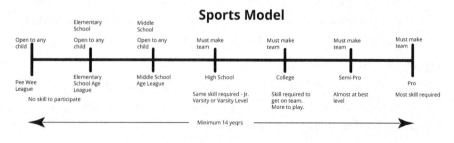

THE TEACHER/COACH

Teachers and coaches also have standards. In order to teach, a teacher must have the proper credentials, and credentials change based upon the level of education. To be a coach, you must have a proven track record. Just about any father can coach a team in the Peewee League by showing up. But even there, things are changing. Recently, because of the dangers of concussion, a USA Football certification was established[32] that a dad can get, ensuring he is properly trained to safely coach football in the Pee-wee League. As a coach progresses in the industry, from the little guys to high school to college and finally to the pros, it becomes more and more important that the coach has a proven track record.

What challenges people about an industry is that there are always flaws in it. But without standards and boundaries, there is no accountability; and thus no ability to understand proficiency or competency in any league or industry. This can be a Catch-22 for those working in the church. Boundaries are necessary but, if we enforce them rigidly, we are considered legalistic; on the other hand, if we are too sloppy, we are considered negligent. We must graciously enforce proper boundaries. Don't you think this subject is important to the proper functioning of the body of Christ as well as the health of the individual believer?

NOW CONSIDER OUR INDUSTRY

When someone enters the Protestant church, it is the same as a kid entering a school at some level. I say at some level because there is nothing mandatory about this industry: people come and go as they wish. There is no age and no agreed upon time frame. While there are standards, they are inconsistent. Let's look at the obvious ones first.

The first choice we make is our denomination; it's our first filter. At some point we have to choose from thousands of different denominations,[33] the most popular being a choice of the following: Baptist, Lutheran, Methodist, Presbyterian, Pentecostal, Congregationalist, Evangelical, Nondenominational.[34] Denominations differ on many areas in theology and practice, such as: the inerrancy of the Bible, baptism, Communion, God's control over the world, the Trinity, women in leadership, the role of

32. "Heads Up Football | Youth Football | USA Football | Football's National Governing Body." Heads Up Football | Youth Football | USA Football | Football's National Governing Body. Accessed October 1, 2015.
33. "List of Christian Denominations." Wikipedia. Accessed October 1, 2015.
34. Being nondenominational simply means you prefer your own accountability. Therefore there is one church in your denomination, your own church.

gay or lesbian leaders, same-sex marriages, and the acceptance and belief in creeds, to name a few.[35]

CHOICE OF A CHURCH

Churches come in various shapes and sizes: some are traditional, some are contemporary, some are held in a home, others in buildings of various sizes, some even in former sports arenas. It has become important for people to feel comfortable in the church they choose, so people often check out many churches before they select one to be their home church. Since there are over 450,000 churches in the United States, most people have lots of choices. People *can shop* for the right church. And it doesn't need to be right around the corner either, thus expanding our *community*. The church no longer reflects the New Testament model in which they typically met in homes:

> … and to the church that meets in your home: Grace and peace to you from God our Father and the Lord Jesus Christ (Philemon 1:1-3).

In fact, we often leave one community to find another one that is more suitable to our lifestyle. The focus is on feeling "comfortable."

CHOICES REGARDING JESUS

Once we've chosen a church, a standardized test for some churches is our ability to understand the Bible and recognize what it teaches about Jesus. Some churches disagree with the fundamentals of Jesus' own teaching. In the churches that do teach the truth about Jesus, we have to decide whether we, as individuals, believe Jesus is God. Jesus asks in Mark 8:29: "Who do you say that I am?" Just like His disciples, we need to answer that question too. If we believe He is the Lord and Savior, we move on in the industry (or at least in my example).

Baptism is an action we take in response to putting our faith in Jesus, thus it becomes a step. Some denominations believe in only one baptism while others believe one must be baptized as a professed believer rather than as a child. Others believe in another baptism, by the Holy Spirit. Some form of prayer is a step in this process. Communion is another step. Once we become a professed Christian, we are also considered a disciple of Christ. That means we are following and learning from our Lord and Savior. One way we do this is by reading and studying the Bible.

Next, we may become a member of the church we have been attending, if membership is offered. Some churches offer membership, while others don't

---

35. An example is the Apostles Creed: I believe in God, the Father Almighty, Creator of heaven and earth; and in Jesus Christ, His only Son, our Lord: Who was conceived by the Holy Spirit, born of the Virgin Mary; suffered under Pontius Pilate, was crucified, died and was buried. There are also others.

think it is biblical. Then we start tithing. I don't know any church that doesn't teach some form of tithing, but there may be some somewhere. Some people believe the tithe should just go to the church while others believe it needs to go to God's work, which may or may not be the local church. This is where the issue of "the body of Christ" gets shaded. Below is a diagram that may represent the typical churchgoer in a typical growing Protestant church.

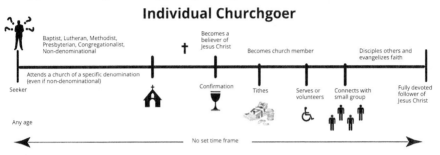

SERVE

Next, we may serve as part of the body of Christ, volunteering our time and involving ourselves in church affairs. Most churches need a variety of help in numerous areas, including: children's ministry, outreach, community affairs, youth ministry, worship, and missions. I became a Sunday school teacher of fifth-graders at my church in Alexandria. I have been involved in church affairs ever since—well, until I didn't fit into the industry's model. But whether someone becomes an usher, greeter, or Sunday school teacher, or helps with the soundboard on a Sunday morning is not the point. The point is that we get involved at this point or we stop moving forward in the process. There is no specific and consistent process for finding and placing volunteers.

SMALL GROUPS

Many churches today, perhaps most, want their body attending small groups. In fact, some churches don't perform Communion in church anymore; instead they instruct their members to do that in their small groups. Small groups have taken over the concept of discipleship for the larger churches, because most large churches realize they cannot effectively disciple their large flock with their own small leadership team. When we start sharing our faith in small groups and making disciples of others, we are completing this part of the typical Protestant process. The Sunday corporate meeting is viewed as a celebration of sorts and it is not expected to meet the needs of discipleship in churches based on this model.

SPIRITUAL GIFTS

Many Christians believe we have spiritual gifts—something the Bible testifies to as well:

A spiritual gift is given to each of us (1 Corinthians 12:7). See also 1 Corinthians 12:1, 4.

God made us all unique and uses us as *one body in the local church*.[36] Similar to the way God picks our parents, He also picks our gifts. Therefore discovering our gifts and using them is an important step in our spiritual walk:

Do not neglect your gift … (1 Timothy 4:14a).

Each one should use whatever gift he has received to serve others … (1 Peter 4:10a).

Some churches do not have a place for members to discover their gifts. Others don't believe in them. That does not mean the local church won't have a place for a member to volunteer; normally it will find a place to put someone. That is why I was able to teach Sunday school before I was a believer without the church knowing anything about my faith or my spiritual gifts. They just needed to fill that spot.

INDIVIDUAL CALLING

In addition to our spiritual gifts, we were also made by God for a specific purpose. The parable about remaining watchful indicates that each of us has an assigned task:

It's like a man going away: He leaves his house and puts his servants in charge, each with his assigned task ... (Mark 13:34).

We have the gifts that go along with our calling. Paul knew his role wasn't to *fit in* where there was a gap in the work (Romans 15:20), although that might have been a part of his earlier training and may be part of ours as well. Paul knew he was chosen to preach the gospel to the Gentiles because Jesus said so. He had specific orders:

Go! This man is my chosen instrument to proclaim my name to the Gentiles and their kings and to the people of Israel (Acts 9:15).

---

36. See 1 Corinthians 12:27-28.

HOW ABOUT US?

Now consider the aforementioned questions from a different angle:

- Are the right people in the right positions in our churches as if we were a professional football team?

- How do we know?

- Are the right people being supported?

- How do we know?

- Is our small-group model filled with qualified leaders?

- How do we know?

- Are we taking advantage of the body of Christ in our midst?

- How do we know?

- Are the parachurch leaders or missionaries in our body properly supported?

- How do we know?

Outside of our staff, filling a need with someone, anyone who does not have a criminal record and has experience in the area we are seeking, may be a good step but, for a professional team, it is a substandard decision. So is trusting someone who has been gifted and called to fill a role without some sort of affirmation process. But in most churches, this is how we currently operate.

PAID STAFF

The only place this seems to be taken seriously is with those who want to be paid staff, such as church leaders. Church leaders participate in the necessary training with its educational requirements (degrees, etc.) so that they are prepared for the work and evaluated. But what about the army these other leaders are in charge of discipling that are not on staff? Shouldn't there be a process that is part of the lives of every disciple of the church to maintain the church's credibility? I know—it is different to work with volunteers who may not be that committed, but if we want to win this war we find ourselves fighting, we need to change.

MY BELIEF

If it is true that most people really do die with their dreams still in them, as I heard a speaker say years ago, and if there is no consistent place in the local church for people to discover their God-given calling or be affirmed or challenged in the calling process, and then no support to fulfill that God-given calling because of the aforementioned gaps in our industry, *then we may have the wrong people in the wrong positions in many of our churches and parachurches.* How many people do you know that are certain of their God-given calling?

Be honest.

How can they be sure whether their choices are God-driven or feelings-driven? How many of them are affirmed by someone credible enough and close enough to them to know? If that number is low, then how can we be sure they are called to be doing what we have asked them to do or that they have decided to do?

Would you feel comfortable boarding an airplane without being certain that your pilot had specific credentials, training, and experience?

I know. Flying a plane is different. But aren't we supposed to be soldiers in a Christian army?

HOW DO WE DECIDE WHOM TO SUPPORT?

That said, and transitioning to the parachurch model, we might be supporting the wrong organizations—never even knowing if the leaders running these supposed Christian organizations are called, qualified or equipped to lead them. I am ordained under the Evangelical Church Alliance (ECA). I had to qualify, and my education and experience mattered. And each year I have to fill out a report letting the ECA know whether or not I am following their guidelines. Shouldn't that matter? If we are focused on business results we may have no idea whether these organizations are God-led or feelings-led:

• Are our parachurch leaders accountable to biblical behavior?
• If so, by whom?
• How about the board of directors of the organizations we support—are they even Christians?
• Do we think this even matters if they are legal and appear to be doing good work for the kingdom?

It appears to me that we base many of our decisions about support either using random, inconsistent, inconclusive opinions or based upon businesslike qualifications that may not accurately reflect Christian values or objectives. We are putting Band-Aids on areas where surgery is needed because we don't have an evaluation process that reveals the root issues we need to address in our work. My experience tells me we are so busy chasing numbers that our ability to even know the answer to these questions is greatly curtailed. I will get more specific when we come to solutions, but for now consider the following graphic as a potential church model:

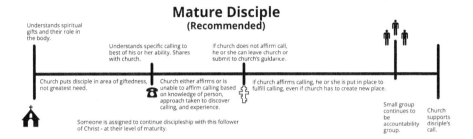

HINDSIGHT IS 20/20

Using my example: That does not mean or imply everyone would have had to understand all the details of my calling, but it would have meant the church was my partner through the process. That partnership would mean budgeting the work according to the specific and agreed upon mission of Hoskins Park Ministries (HPM). Then, as the steps of my calling were revealed, the church would have worked with me through the challenges I faced as part of the body of Christ. Once I realized the need for additional "disciplers" for the staff of HPM, the church would have assessed that cost and assisted in a solution. If at any point the church felt it was no longer called to support me, or able to support me, for whatever reason, then we would have had a discussion. And I would have a choice: To keep going in a direction I felt was God-led, without their full support, or to stop. The process would have been the same with other churches I approached. This would have kept the process of discipleship in- tact from church to church, particularly if the churches became more collaborative. I would not have been left to myself, suddenly on my own with no accountability with the church wondering what, if anything, it had to do with them.

This process would also keep people who want to start another church or parachurch from just doing it without some process that affirms or denies their so-called "calling." If they chose to move out of the parameters being discussed, supporters would know it before they enabled them to do something as the Lone Ranger. This process would require unity and real discipleship over the body. Sound impossible? You're right! In our strength it is—but not in God's:

Jesus looked at them and said, "With man this is impossible, but with God all things are possible" (Matthew 19:26).

If we don't re-assess our assessment process, we may starve some of our best leaders and enable some of our least mature or least experienced ones.

Kings and rulers make a grave mistake when they give great authority to foolish people and low positions to people of proven worth (Ecclesiastes 10:5-6).

CHAPTER 12
QUESTIONS

1. What did you glean from the education, business, and sports models? What do they have in common?

2. What would happen if accountability were taken out of your work?

3. Do you hold anyone accountable? What is the purpose?

4. Do you have a general idea how much time coaches, mentors, tutors, teachers, and parents spend with their athletes, students or kids? Why do you think they spend that much time with them?

5. Who are you teaching? How much time does that take?

6. Do you know of any professional athlete/team that does not have a coach investing large amounts of time with them? Why do you think that is? How does this connect with our topic?

13 The Final AHA Moment— Shallow Discipleship

"'What sorrow awaits the leaders of my people—the shepherds of my sheep—for they have destroyed and scattered the very ones they were expected to care for' says the Lord."
—Jeremiah 23:1 NLT

My fifth and final AHA moment was the big one. It is the root of all the others. When our discipleship process does not reveal callings and when there is not a deep level of discipleship in the local church to support the revealed callings of the body of Christ, the entire model falls apart. One of the results of this is that despite our best efforts, we are often allowing our most trained and perhaps most dedicated soldiers to fight a war getting only our crumbs, while some of our least-trained and experienced soldiers are fully funded because they focus on business results. The fifth AHA moment is the shallow discipleship process in our local churches that prevents us from ensuring we have the most qualified army leading the way.

COMMON TRAITS

While there are variations in mentoring, teaching, sponsoring, coaching, parenting, and training, most understand its importance in life. Everyone needs a positive influence in his or her life in order to be a positive influence in society. This is particularly true when we are broken. As Marvin Olasky writes:

> Often when a life is broken, it can only be rebuilt by another caring, concerned human being. Someone whose actions say, "I love you, I believe in you, I'm in your corner." This is compassion with a human face and a human voice. It is not an isolated act—it is a personal relationship. And it works.[37]

By definition, mentoring, tutoring, shepherding, teaching, and discipling are the same, but is the same amount of time, effort, skill, and assessment part of the discipleship process in our churches? Most churches have a discipleship

---

37. Olasky, Marvin N. *Compassionate Conservatism: What It Is, What It Does, and How It Can Transform America*. New York: Free Press, 2000. 217.

process, of course; some are more formal than others, but most do not have a consistent standard to measure success. As previously discussed, this process is arbitrary, random, inconclusive, and dependent upon busy people's participation.

PROPER TEACHERS AND STUDENTS

The movie, *Chasing Mavericks,* the true story of Jay Moriarty, is an extreme example about proper teachers and students.[38] Jay Moriarty wanted to surf the largest waves in the world, called mavericks. He met someone who surfed those waves, Frosty Hesson, and he begged Frosty to coach him. Frosty knew Jay, who was sixteen and a fantastic surfer, but surfing 50-plus foot waves is dangerous. Waves that size kill well-intended surfers since the pressure of the water is so great that if the surfer falls while riding one of those waves or attempting to do so, it can smash the surfer into the bottom with enough force to kill or drown him. Metaphorically speaking, this is similar to a Christian wanting to help the homeless or those living in a culture of poverty in a meaningful way. It may appear to be "surfing" but these waves can kill you. He told Jay no, he would not train him. Frosty's wife, knowing Jay was really his protégé, told him that Jay was going to attempt to ride those waves whether Frosty trained him or not. Reluctantly, Frosty agreed and gave Jay two unalterable goals and one ultimatum before they would even get in the water with those big waves. Here were the two goals:

1. Jay needed to successfully paddle the twenty-something-mile stretch from Santa Cruz to Monterey Bay; and

2. Jay had to hold his breath for 4 minutes.

Those were the two prerequisites. The ultimatum was that Jay had to do everything he was told to do by Frosty, no matter what, without question or attitude. Jay agreed to the terms and conditions of the coach.

WHY THESE GOALS?

Why these two goals and the ultimatum? In order for Jay to successfully paddle the long stretch from Santa Cruz to Monterey, Frosty knew he would have to be in great physical condition. He would also have to study the tides and understand the currents in order to succeed, since fighting a current would prevent him from making the trek. Therefore, built into the first goal, which appeared to be about fitness, was another important goal: mental assessment of the ocean. This was necessary for Jay to surf mavericks and survive

---

38. *Chasing Mavericks.* Directed by Curtis Hanson. Twentieth Century Fox Home Entertainment [éd.]: 2013. Film.

fast-changing conditions. The second goal was strictly for survival. Frosty knew that even if Jay was unable to catch one of the monster waves, if he could hold his breath for four minutes he would likely survive his attempts to do so. The ultimatum simply saved time by eliminating the needless discussions that may have surrounded a request Frosty would make of Jay without Jay understanding its purpose. It's like a parent trying to explain something to a child who just isn't old, wise, or experienced enough to understand. Jay did what he was told, Frosty held his hand through the process, and Jay ended up riding some of the largest waves in the world. In fact, Jay is featured on the cover of *Surfer Magazine,* May, 1995.[39]

WHAT WE LEARN

This story emphasizes:

1. The need to have students like Jay who want to reach their greatest potential

2. The need to have experienced leaders—people like Frosty who are capable of teaching someone like Jay and who make themselves available to teach

3. The need to have students *who are willing* to do what their teacher tells them to do in order to achieve their potential

The Bible says:

> Students are not greater than their teacher. But the student who is fully trained will become like the teacher (Luke 6:40).

We need to have experienced teachers like Frosty and eager students like Jay that both realize the importance of the other and are willing to commit to the relationship. This is particularly true when we engage the poor.

But do we?

WILLOW CREEK

Willow Creek Church, one of the largest churches in the United States, did some research to determine if they were effectively discipling their body. The REVEAL study they undertook in 2004 taught them they were good at selling people on Christianity but not as good in dealing with those who were the most sold. The more mature Christians in their body felt they received the least amount of support by their church's leadership team. Using the

---

39. "Surfer Magazine Jay Moriarty Wipeout Cover Photo." HistoryvsHollywood.com. Accessed October 22, 2015.

education model from the previous chapter as a metaphor, a person in our church who is graduating from college and wants to get a Master's degree or Doctorate, cannot find anyone qualified or that has the time to teach at that level unless we engage in the formal educational process that does not include discipleship: There is no "Frosty" to teach "Jay" how to surf mavericks. Even with our eternity at stake.

John Maxwell clarifies this from a business perspective in his book *Developing the Leaders Around You.*[40] He points out the importance of developing the leaders God has put in one's life before the organization can grow. And this can't just happen with the leaders on staff at our churches if we want more soldiers in our army. We need to consider parachurch leaders as our adopted leaders and disciple them while they disciple others. We also need to consider small-group leaders in the body who are not paid staff.

> Therefore, this is what the Lord, the God of Israel, says to these shepherds: "Instead of caring for my flock and leading them to safety, you have deserted them ..." But I will gather together the remnant of my flock from the countries where I have driven them. I will bring them back to their own sheepfold, and they will be fruitful and increase in number. Then I will appoint responsible shepherds who will care for them, and they will never be afraid again. Not a single one will be lost or missing. I, the Lord, have spoken! (Jeremiah 23:2-4).

> Harsh words. I know. But we need to take them seriously.

DISCIPLE EVERYONE

Irrespective of whether someone is a leader or not, we must disciple our entire body. That includes the gamut of believers from our youngest and least mature, to the oldest and most mature. And the process cannot stop at a random point in the process because we don't have the maturity of leaders to keep the process advancing. When and if we see a break in this process: whether it is someone who rejects discipleship or someone we reject because our most mature leaders are not mature enough or are too "busy" to disciple a maturing believer who is asking for discipleship, we need to investigate the obstacle and fix it. And we may have to turn our church upside down to do so.

If discipleship is our true call, we must value it above all else without forgetting it is the foundation for evangelism. Our best evangelists are not

40. Maxwell, John C. *Developing the Leaders Around You.* Nashville, Tenn.: T. Nelson, 1995.

the ones talking the talk; they are walking the walk. Discipleship is the only process that will ensure that result.

So there you have it, my five AHA moments:

1. Unrealistic expectations for those I wanted to help

2. Misunderstanding the parachurch model that I was part of

3. Fragmentation of the Christian army over money

4. Discovery of the mysterious, but real, Christian industry

5. A shallow and busy discipleship process in our local churches hampering our effectiveness

I find myself where I am today because of those issues that caught me off-guard when I moved into "the hood" all those years ago.

Part III of *Would You Have Fired Judas?* addresses solutions to these AHA moments. If we did the following, they would disappear:

1. Assessed our leaders and congregants more accurately and consistently

2. Assessed the groups in our churches or parachurches using criteria that is fundamental to a successful group

3. Deepened the actual process of discipleship by spending more time with fewer people

4. Had a process to help someone discover their individual calling as best they could

5. Helped folks know who God is calling them to disciple

6. Stopped shooting our wounded and instead, helped them recover through an agreed upon process

7. Had a more efficient process for putting the right people in the right leadership positions in our churches and parachurches

It is to these solutions we now turn.

CHAPTER 13
QUESTIONS

1. Have you ever had a mentor or tutor? How did they help you?

2. When has it been important for you to be taught by an expert? What process did you undertake to determine who had the expertise to teach you?

3. If you got on an airplane, would you care whether your pilot had the proper training? Most of us assume our pilots are trained because they are in an industry that demands it, right?

4. If a leader does not have the normal, required, or typical degree(s), what should be the assessment process to ensure that leader is equipped to lead?

5. When your money or life is at stake, how important is the research, training, education, and assessment of the person who is sharing their opinion with you?

6. How important is your eternity? Who is teaching you about the afterlife? What training do they have? Who is teaching about poverty? What training do they have?

THE SOLUTIONS

WHAT NEEDS TO CHANGE
IN OUR CHRISTIAN
INSTITUTIONS IF WE WANT
TO IMPACT THE DARKNESS
WE FIND OURSELVES
IN TODAY

14 Reality Check: Keeping It Real Through Assessment

"Examine yourselves to see whether you are in the faith; test yourselves. Do you not realize that Christ Jesus is in you—unless, of course, you fail the test?"
—2 Corinthians 13:5

The first solution to the aforementioned AHA moments is having a biblical process of assessment of our Christian army. Oftentimes Christians expect other people to give up their bad habits while thinking their own behavior is okay. That is wrong thinking and the kind of hypocrisy that keeps outsiders "out."

It's time we all took a good look at the man or woman we see in the mirror. It is time we examined our faith to see if it is genuine. We need to be fruit inspectors.

> By their fruit you will recognize them. Do people pick grapes from thornbushes, or figs from thistles? Likewise, every good tree bears good fruit, but a bad tree bears bad fruit. A good tree cannot bear bad fruit, and a bad tree cannot bear good fruit. Every tree that does not bear good fruit is cut down and thrown into the fire. Thus, by their fruit you will recognize them (Matthew 7:15-20).

But how do we do that in a gracious but concrete manner? We look to the Scriptures! Assessment need not scare or deter us, but it needs to be based upon God's Word. I have also added ways to make it relevant to our culture. Since God's sheep can hear His voice (John 10:27), I trust you will use discernment as you progress through this process.

COACH SMITH

In his book *It's How You Play The Game*, David Chadwick discusses the success of University of North Carolina basketball coach Dean Smith. One of the important points Pastor Chadwick makes about Coach Smith was that he knew each of his players well—well enough to understand their talent with a basketball, their personality, their unique psychological makeup, and their limitations. All of these factors matter—more so in a game.

According to Pastor Chadwick, Coach Smith would regularly shout out, "Know your limits!" in practice so that players would depend on the team to win a game, rather than an unrealistic assessment of their own skills.[41] Coach Smith knew his players. We must know our disciples—starting with the man or woman in the mirror. We must also know our leaders before putting them into leadership positions.

STAGES

A Christian has to *be a disciple* before he or she can teach others to do the same. We don't accept Jesus Christ and become His best students overnight. There is a process we go through as we become fully devoted followers of Christ.

A process. Let's not forget that. And a process is different than a formula. This should encourage us to consider our progress whether we are looking in the mirror or standing on a scale. Neither the mirror nor the scale condemns; they merely reveal truth. That is the purpose of this *subjective* evaluation—to keep it real. Any misinterpretation of this would not only completely miss the point and purpose, but would be legalistic and judgmental. This is not our intent:

> For it is by grace you have been saved, through faith—and this is not from yourselves, it is the gift of God—not by works, so that no one can boast (Ephesians 2:8-9).

We must have an intimate relationship with Christ and keep our eyes on him so that we can hear from Him.[42] Consider this process as *a way* to hear from him.[43] It is not my intent to assume a linear process. In fact, I don't think the process is linear at all. It has not been for me as I have implied. But that cannot excuse us from taking account of where we are "today."

Consider these seven stages as an example of a way the average American Christian can see where they are in this process.

1. Commitment, repentance, and adjustments

---

41. Chadwick, David. *It's How You Play the Game: The 12 Leadership Principles of Dean Smith*. Eugene, Ore.: Harvest House, 2015. 105.

42. Wilson, Carl W. *With Christ in the School of Disciple Building: A Study of Christ's Method of Building Disciples*. Colorado Springs, Colo. : NavPress, 2009. Also see, http://toi.edu/Training%20Materials/leading%20spiritual%20movements/Student%20Notes/E9Discipleship%20Assessment.pdf

43. This list is adapted from Pastor Tompkins' seven stages. Tompkins, Jim. "The Biblical Process of Discipleship." Loving the Word with the MudPreacher. July 27, 2012. Accessed October 1, 2015.

2. Development, guidance, and involvement: "learning about the One who gave me new life"

3. Growth in the body of Christ and personal discernment

4. Ministry development and testing

5. Further testing: "learning to depend on Christ"

6. Ministry in the power of Christ

7. Maturity in Christ: "fruit through the fullness of Christ"

TIME FRAME & ASSUMPTIONS

I am suggesting a timeframe of 14-plus years (minimum) to complete stages one through six (taking two-four years per stage). This is based on our education model, which takes twenty-five years to fully complete; the sports model, which requires fourteen years; and these biblical characters:

Moses waited forty years. Abraham waited thirty. Joseph waited thirteen years. David ten. Paul spent at least fourteen years being trained. Jesus was thirty when He began His ministry.

I am also making a few other assumptions throughout the entire process. These assumptions are that the disciple is typically:

• A true believer—someone committed to the essentials of the faith and who does not believe sin is subjective to individual interpretation (2 Peter 1:20—if this is even a question it is likely the person does not fit my definition)

• In a community (small group) of Christians that share life together (Hebrews 10:25)

• Regularly meeting with an accountability partner who asks specific questions in their areas of struggle (James 5:16)

• Not dealing with addictions on a daily basis (1 John 3:6 / Hebrews 10:26). (In the first stages, they may be *struggling* against addictions, but it should no longer be a daily issue)

• Someone that understands a follower of Jesus lives a righteous life and loves others using the biblical definition of love found in 1 Corinthians 13:4-8. There are various scriptures to support this assumption but I will refer to this one:

Stages of Discipleship	Non-believer Stage Zero	Immature believer Stage One	Immature believer Stage Two	Mature believer Stage Three
Time (est./subjective min.)	All the years prior to stage one.	2-4 years	4-6 years a Christian	6-8 years a Christian
Stage Principle	Unsure of life. Questioning beliefs. Seeking Truth.	Commitment to Christ, repentance of egregious sin & adjustment of relationships.	Development of Christian beliefs, guidance from Holy Spirit & involvement in ministry.	Growth in Christ & personal discernment of spiritual matters.
Calling	Life is self-focused. All talents are used to promote self.	Understanding spiritual gifts. Calling centers on change of behavior.	Growing inclination towards kingdom service.	Involved in God's work. Discerning calling through experience.
Understanding/ Issues re: Sin	Sin is breaking the man made laws of the culture. Has nothing to do with the Bible.	Have repented of egregious sin. Some Pharisaical tendencies can develop like a repented smoker.	Tendency from self-righteousness to someone who is tolerant of all sin (sloppy agape). Sin is compared to man (not God).	Start to realize our own sin as we are humbled by life's challenges. No daily addictions.
% living Flesh/spirit	100% in the flesh	49% flesh/51% spirit	45% flesh/55% spirit	40% flesh/60% spirit
Disciplines	May pray but not sure to whom.	Praying and reading the Bible.	Praying, studying the Bible, try fasting.	Praying, studying, regularly & inconsistent fasting.
Physical Counter	Spiritually unborn.	Infant. Born Again.	Child ("me" centered)	Teenager
Educational Equivalent		Kindergarten	Elementary School	Middle School
+ Behavior		Excited about faith. Fresh.	Righteous.	Faithful, Risk Taking, Trusting.
- Behavior	Worldly. Self-Focused. Be happy.	Confident. ← Overbearing.	Judgmental.	Operating in flesh. Pride.
Supporting Scriptures	Romans 5:10	2 Corinthians 7:10, Acts 26:20	Romans 5:10	Ephesians 4:14-16, Romans 8:29
Prominent Scripture	In those days Israel had no king; all the people did whatever seemed right in their own eyes (Judges 17:16).	Jesus replied, 'I tell you the truth, unless you are born again, you cannot see the Kingdom of God' (John 3:3).	In those days Israel had no king; all the people did whatever seemed right in their own eyes (Judges 17:16).	Grow in the grace and knowledge of our Lord & Savior Jesus Christ (2 Peter 3:18)

114

Mature believer Stage Four	Mature believer Stage Five	Mature believer Stage Six	Mature believer Stage Seven
8-10 years a Christian	10-12 years a Christian	12-14 years a Christian	14 years+
Ministry discernment / development & testing.	Increased discernment, further testing, revelation of blind spots.	Advanced refinement, testing, & dependence.	Final engagement and maturity.
Know calling & pursuing.	Death of a vision to resurrection and restoration.	Known and pursuing affirmed calling in power of Holy Spirit.	Fully engaged. Maturing.
Because of spiritual warfare, tempted back to old habits. Challenged by complacency and cynicism. Definition of sin being tested.	Not just talking the talk but walking the walk. Living righteous life as defined by the Holy Bible.	Like Paul, worst of sinners. But that is compared to God - not man. Understands even more the need for Jesus.	Fully dependent on God's grace to cover sinful man. Living righteous life.
30% flesh/70% spirit	10% flesh/80% spirit	15% flesh/85% spirit	10% flesh/90% spirit
Praying, studying, is daily routine. Regularly fast.	Constantly praying, reading, studying Word, fasting.	Praying, reading, studying, fasting is a way of life.	
Young adult	Adult	Parent	Grandparent
High School	College	Graduate school	Doctorate
Humility, Boldness. Spiritual warfare ➤ Struggling	Patience. Humility. Impatience. Pride.	Balanced	It's all about grace.
Complacency.			
Philippians 1:9-10, 1 Corinthians 3:6-9, Jeremiah 29:11	Jonah 2:8, Hebrews 12:5-7, 1 Peter 4:12-14	Philippians 1:6, Romans 8:28, 1 Corinthians 2:3	John 15:4-5, Colossians 1:5-6
To become perfect and mature, lacking nothing, we must have patience (James 1:4).	These trials will show that your faith is genuine. It is being tested as fire tests and purifies gold—through your faith is far more precoius than mere gold. So when your faith remains strong through many trials, it will bring you much praise and glory and honor on the day when Jesus Christ is revealed to the whole world (1 Peter 1:6-7).		I have not achieved it, but I focus on this one thing: Forgetting the past and looking forward to what lies ahead, I press on to reach the end of the race and receive the heavenly prize for which God, through Christ Jesus, is calling us (Philippians 3:13-14).

This is how we know who the children of God are and who the children of the devil are: Anyone who does not do what is right is not God's child, nor is anyone who does not love their brother and sister (1 John 3:10).

PREREQUISITES

A believer may be without a small group, or an accountability partner, or a community for a time. If this continued for an extended period of time, it would be a setback and could cause a potential reversal in stages or a freeze in the current stage. If a believer backslides back into an addiction, the stage stops. It will revert to stage one or two if the believer does not take steps to eradicate the addiction over the course of the year. (One can only struggle against an addiction for so long before one needs to be freed from it; otherwise we are saying God's strength is not enough for us to conquer our idol.) Typically, however, this will not be a factor since an accountability partner and strong community keep matters from reaching this point. This usually happens to Lone Ranger Christians, which is why this process is being discussed—to assure discipleship is being accomplished with our disciples and that there are no Lone Ranger Christians.

CATEGORIES

We will assess each stage using the following criteria: time, the disciple's calling, sin, behavior, and relevant Scriptures. I have added a physical and educational equivalent for comparison purposes. Since we are souls with skin on us, I took a shot at evaluating us from the perspective of how much of our Christian lives should be lived in the flesh versus the Spirit or, said another way, how disciplined we are with the life God has given us. Disciples are disciplined. We have the Holy Spirit inside of us. This category monitors our progress. The Bible says if we are living the majority of our Christian life (51% as a minimum) by the Spirit of God, we are considered His children (Romans 8:12-14).[44] The number listed for each stage is a subjective maximum amount that the disciple should be living according to his or her flesh.

These comparisons are meant to make the same point: there are changes we have to make as Christians in order to advance. *They matter once we get to a place where we may be put in leadership in a ministry.* I have included questions for you to consider throughout the process to see if your life/behavior reflects

---

44. Therefore, brothers and sisters, we have an obligation—but it is not to the flesh, to live according to it. For if you live according to the flesh, you will die; but if by the Spirit you put to death the misdeeds of the body, you will live. For those who are led by the Spirit of God are the children of God (Romans 8:12-14).

the stage. Take a look at the chart on pages 114 and 115 and see if you can find out where you fit best today. Then read about the different stages and see if you can accurately assess yourself.

Stage Zero—Seeker

Stage principles: Unsure of life. Questioning beliefs. Seeking truth. God is pursuing.

Time: All the years prior to stage one.

Calling: Life is lived selfishly as part of the culture with a worldly mindset. Gifts are understood as areas of interest. Gifts are developed, targets are made, but without understanding the reason for the gifts or the inclination to do one thing or another.

Sin: Sin is equated with the legal system. What is right and wrong is found in the justice system (our government) although our conscience is still God-wired. Our culture has a major impact on our understanding of sin over the long haul. That means it becomes a moving target. We don't really care what another person thinks as long as it doesn't directly impact us.

Percent living in flesh: 100%

Physical counter: Unborn. Spiritually dead. Enemies of God.

+ / - Behavior: Worldly. Self-focused. Be happy; it is your right.

Supporting Scriptures: Colossians 1:21 NLT: *You were his enemies, separated from him by your evil thoughts and actions.* Romans 5:10: *For since our friendship with God was restored by the death of his Son while we were still his enemies, we will certainly be saved through the life of his Son.*

Prominent Scripture: *In those days Israel had no king; all the people did whatever seemed right in their own eyes* (Judges 17:6).

SELFISH LIVING

For most of my life I lived for myself. I believed the adage, "He who dies with the most toys wins." According to the Bible, I was an enemy of God, yet He pursued me. I have countless spiritual markers in my life that show God revealing Himself to me. Years before I became a Christian, I found a small, cheap, beat-up plastic cross on the ground. I could not pass it by. I still have it today, twenty-five years later. I have many of these spiritual markers during the secular part of my journey. Then, through many trials in life, I came to the end of myself and changed directions. I began to understand that we live in a real-life "matrix" with the visible and invisible world:

> And Elisha prayed, 'Open his eyes, Lord, so that he may see.' Then the Lord opened the servant's eyes, and he looked and saw the hills full of horses and chariots of fire all around Elisha (2 Kings 6:17).

THE MATRIX

A great movie that underscores my point is *The Matrix*.[45] Thomas Anderson, played by Keanu Reeves, is a professional computer programmer during the day and at night becomes a computer hacker known as "Neo" who questions the reality of life—at least as he knows it. He knows what he sees everyday: people living their lives as doctors, lawyers, professionals, preachers and so on. Deep down, he senses something is wrong, he just cannot put his finger on what it is. He is living life without any purpose beyond self-satisfaction. A soldier (Morpheus), who knows the truth and who is fighting for freedom for his people, contacts Neo. Morpheus, in an effort to recruit Neo, tells him what the matrix is—a façade, or cover over reality. Then he tells him about the real world, a war that rages behind the artificial matrix between humanity and machines. He tells Neo that he believes Neo is supposed to be fighting in this war. In fact, he tells him that without Neo they will not have a chance of winning it. Neo ultimately has a choice: to accept this new reality or choose to live in a lie about daily life. He makes his irreversible choice by taking a blue pill offered to him by Morpheus and joining the team of people who are fighting the agents—machines that look like people but are really the enemy.

BIBLICAL SIMILARITY

Biblically, there is a similarity to this, but it is not about man and machines; it is about the physical world which we can see and the spiritual one which we cannot. We can either choose to follow God or live as we like. Following God is a narrow path, according to Matthew 7:13, full of discomfort and sacrifice. Living as we like requires denying that this other "hidden" world exists. This stage is deciding whether to take the red pill or the blue one. When we decide to take the blue pill we move on to the first stage.

> So we fix our eyes not on what is seen, but on what is unseen, since what is seen is temporary, but what is unseen is eternal (Corinthians 4:18).

45. *The Matrix*. Directed by Andy Wachowski. Warner Bros. Pictures: 2001. Film.

Stage One—Commitment, Repentance & Adjustment

Stage principles: Commitment to Christ, repentance of obvious sin, and adjustment of relationships.

Minimum Time: 2-4 years in this stage.

Calling: Understanding spiritual gifts.

Sin: Conspicuously sinful behavior stops. Some Pharisaical tendencies may develop as the new Christian doesn't understand the extent of their non-egregious sin.

Max. percent living in flesh: 49%

Physical counter: Infant / born-again (me centered)[46]

+ / - Behavior: Excited. Fresh. Overbearing. Most have a confidence in their new faith.

Supporting Scriptures: 2 Corinthians 7:10, Acts 26:20.

Prominent Scripture: John 3:3: *No one can see the kingdom of God unless they are born again.*

COMMITMENT

I accepted Christ into my heart at Forest Hill Church in the spring of 1994. I made a decision to give up my old life—all those things the Bible said were not honoring Jesus——and I put my faith in Jesus Christ as my Lord and Savior. I invited Jesus Christ to "take the wheel," as Carrie Underwood sings in her song of the same name. When I did this, I was miraculously and mysteriously saved. The Bible says:

> When the people heard this, they were cut to the heart and said to Peter and the other apostles, "Brothers, what shall we do?" Peter replied, "Repent and be baptized, every one of you, in the name of Jesus Christ for the forgiveness of your sins. And you will receive the gift of the Holy Spirit" (Acts 2:37-38).

I understood I was a sinner in need of a Savior (Romans 3:10), and I committed my life to Jesus (John 3:16).

---

46. "3 STAGES OF DISCIPLESHIP DB—DSM500STUDYNOTES." 3 STAGES OF DISCIPLESHIP DB—DSM500STUDYNOTES. Accessed October 22, 2015.

REPENTANCE AND ADJUSTMENTS

This caused immediate changes in my behavior. Before I met the Lord, I smoked, drank, had premarital sex, looked at pornography, used foul language, and participated in other similar behavior. When I committed my life to Christ, I repented of those things.

I stopped doing them.

This had a domino effect on my relationships. My business partner noticed the change and did not care for this less pushy version of me. Others were turned off by my commitment to Christ because they didn't know this new me. I had exchanged my old life for a new one in Christ—giving up my own sin for God's righteousness. I was a new man:

> Therefore, if anyone is in Christ, the new creation has come: The old has gone, the new is here! (2 Corinthians 5:17)

Because of my commitment to Christ and the change in my behavior, my relationships changed. I got closer to Christians in my life, while there was a natural distancing from those people in my life who were not following Jesus. That was one of the most challenging adjustments of this stage since my community changed:

> Do not be yoked together with unbelievers. For what do righteousness and wickedness have in common? Or what fellowship can light have with darkness? (2 Corinthians 6:14)

I got involved in my church as a volunteer teaching Sunday school to third-graders while also connecting with the singles group. (Note: this was not the experience teaching fifth-graders in Alexandria before I made a commitment to Christ—this was after my commitment.)

QUESTIONS

The following questions should provide further clarification for stage one:

1. From a moral perspective, what behaviors changed in your life when you accepted Jesus as your Lord and Savior?

2. What about your interaction with others?

3. What have you stopped doing or started doing because of your new commitment?

There must be a change. You cannot have the God of the Universe living inside of your through His Spirit without change.

Stage Two—Development, Guidance, and Involvement

Stage principles: Development of Christian beliefs, guidance from Holy Spirit, and involvement in ministry.

Minimum Time: 4-6 years as a born-again Christian.

Calling: Ranges from those who are still unsure of a calling, to those who are feeling an inclination of a specific call, to those who ignore a calling they feel might be on their life. Little experience.

Sin: Tendency to be self-righteous on one extreme (legalistic) to overly tolerant of sin on the other (sloppy agape—misuse of God's grace).

Max. percent living in flesh: 45%

Physical counter: Child (still me-centered)

+ / - Behavior: Ranges from living righteously on one extreme to being judgmental on the other.

Supporting Scriptures: 2 Corinthians 5:21, Romans 5:1, 1 Corinthians 12:9-10.

Prominent Scripture: I *have been crucified with Christ and I no longer live, but Christ lives in me. The life I now live in the body, I live by faith in the Son of God, who loved me and gave himself for me* (Galatians 2:20).

DEVELOPMENT AND GUIDANCE

The second stage in the process is further development, guidance, and involvement in Christ and His work. If we used the education model as a metaphor, we would be in elementary school. We begin to pray more; read or study Scripture at a deeper level; spend more time with other Christians discussing relevant matters from a godly perspective; and we see God answer our prayers in very intimate ways. We are getting to know the One who called us to Himself. We are typically as excited about this new direction in our lives now as we were originally, and have discovered even better ways to share our faith.

Think back on those early days when you first learned about Christ. Remember how you remained faithful even though it meant terrible suffering. Sometimes you were exposed to public ridicule and were beaten, and sometimes you helped others who were suffering the same things. You suffered along with those who were thrown into jail, and when all you owned was taken from you, you accepted it with joy. You knew there were better things waiting for you that will last forever (Hebrews 10:33-34 NLT).

We are open to new ideas and have not matured enough to compromise in our growing beliefs about areas of Christianity that are less familiar to us—such as speaking in tongues, the use of other spiritual gifts, spiritual disciplines like fasting and the gift of healing.

HEALING

At this stage in my own journey I volunteered at a local ministry that provided a weekly lunch for the homeless. During one of my visits I noticed a downtrodden woman who was segregated from the others. Her skin rashes appeared to be the reason most kept their distance. I eventually learned that she was suffering from Lupus, a chronic, autoimmune disease. On one of my subsequent visits I became overwhelmed with a godly love for this hurting and lonely woman. I felt God lead me to take her sore infested hands and pray for her healing.

So I did. I took her by both hands and we prayed.

The next two weeks I returned to the ministry but she was nowhere to be found. I was told she had suffered a heart attack and had been admitted to a local hospital. I was in shock; I had prayed for her healing and she had a heart attack!

That did not stop me from visiting her. When I arrived at the hospital, the previously downtrodden woman lit up like a light at my visit. She told me that because of her heart attack the hospital had provided medication for her Lupus, and the skin sores that were previously so obvious on her hands and arms were completely healed. God used a heart attack to get her treatment for her Lupus. All I needed to do was obey that small voice that told me to pray for her healing—despite any reluctance from my feelings regarding her "disease."

God reveals Himself to us—we just have to have faith that the voice we hear—is His.

GODLY BEHAVIOR

This is also a time when we begin to see some contradictions with what we read in the Bible and what we see in the actions of others. Tests come as we continue to grow in our knowledge and understanding of God's Word. We are open to short-term mission work, perhaps even go on one, and serve Christ on a part-time basis. This stage also means continuous growth in the process of conversion by doing what God tells us to do *in the Bible:*

But why do you call Me, 'Lord, Lord,' and not do the things which I say? (Luke 6:46)

We either tend to be judgmental with some tendencies like the Pharisees of old or we overlook sin for the sake of grace. Our prayer life develops as we understand better what it means that God is our Father in heaven. We continue to hear about grace but might not completely understand what it means as we struggle against legalism.

QUESTIONS
To further assess stage two, answer these questions:

1. Since conversion, how have you matured in your faith?

2. Consider when you made your decision to follow Jesus. Do you remember what you were like then? How have you grown?

3. Are you more involved in the church?

4. Are you participating in a small group?

5. Has your prayer life developed?

6. Do you know more about the Bible?

7. What Scripture verses have sparked your soul?

8. Do you have a growing love for other people? (As you develop through these different stages your love for your neighbor should grow at an escalating rate! That means your level of selfishness should decrease at the same rate!)

If there is no growth, no change, you are still in stage one.

Stage Three—Growth in the Body of Christ & Personal Discernment

Stage principles: Growth in Christ and personal discernment regarding spiritual matters.

Minimum Time: 6-8 years as a committed Christian.

Calling: Our calling is still being clarified or nurtured. Many are still unsure of their specific calling and so are not pursuing.

Sin: Starting to realize we are more of a sinner than we thought!

Max. percent living in flesh: 40%

Physical counter: Teenager (self-centered)

+ / - Behavior: Risk-taking (walking by faith) to operating in the flesh through pride.

Supporting Scriptures: Ephesians 4:14-16, Romans 8:29.

Prominent Scripture: *Grow in the grace and knowledge of our Lord and Savior Jesus Christ* (2 Peter 3:18). *Exercise yourself toward godliness* (1 Timothy 4:7).

GROWTH

This stage is marked by further growth in our Christian character. Consider this a middle school or junior high on the educational continuum. We continue to learn more about the Bible and face additional testing of our faith, which humbles our judgmental attitude a bit and molds our character more closely to the character of Christ. It is the beginning of our move from a fundamental understanding of our faith to a practical one.

We see the importance of deepening in our faith. We begin to assess what seed we are as we understand Scriptures like the sower and seed as applicable to our own walk. This parable teaches the different responses of those who hear from God through His Word. The farmer is God, and the seed is His Word. Here is the parable:

A farmer went out to sow his seed. As he was scattering the seed, some fell along the path, and the birds came and ate it up. Some fell on rocky places, where it did not have much soil. It sprang up quickly, because the soil was shallow. But when the sun came up, the plants were scorched, and they withered because they had no root. Other seed fell among thorns, which grew up and choked the plants. Still other seed fell on good soil, where it produced a crop—a hundred, sixty or thirty times what was sown. Whoever has ears, let them hear (Matthew 13:3-9).

MEANING

Here is the explanation Jesus gave to his disciples as to its meaning:

The seed falling on rocky ground refers to someone who hears the word and at once receives it with joy. But since they have no root, they last only a short time. When trouble or persecution comes because of the word, they quickly fall away. The seed falling among the thorns refers to someone who hears the word, but the worries of this life and the deceitfulness of wealth choke the word, making it unfruitful. But the seed falling on good soil refers to someone who hears the word and understands it. This is the one who produces a crop, yielding a hundred, sixty or thirty times what was sown (Matthew 13:20-23).

PERSONAL RELATIONSHIP

I want to explain this from another perspective, a relational one, since most of us are familiar with a relationship "cycle." Typically those of us in Western cultures don't just meet someone and get married. Over time we develop a relationship with another person and then we choose to commit or to move on. Using the parable as our metaphor, the first seed that falls on rocky ground could be likened to meeting someone you are attracted to for the first time. We call that chemistry. It gets the engine burning in a romantic relationship. They are the perfect stranger, since we love the idea of that person rather than loving a person we really don't know. Reality hits when we get to know them at a deeper level. If the relationship makes it through that stage, we begin to deal with the stresses of life. Because of those stresses, we often dismiss the person even if we don't know why. While 90% of adults think stress can negatively impact their health, most don't connect the dots of stress to other areas of their life, like failed relationships. Dr. Larry Crabb, in his book, *The Silence of Adam*, says men under pressure turn to sex and/or violence[47]—both relationship-busters. But if we meet someone, get to know that person, and don't let the stress of life ruin the relationship, the relationship blossoms. It is the same with our relationship with God. For those whose seed falls on good soil, our relationship with God grows and we produce godly results for God's kingdom, whatever our circumstances.

I moved from a part-time to a full-time position with my church. This was also when I had the dream about being lukewarm. At this point we should have a clearer idea of our calling because of our experiences in His work:

For we are God's masterpiece. He has created us anew in Christ Jesus, so we can do the good things he planned for us long ago (Ephesians 2:10).

---

47. Crabb, Lawrence J., and Don Hudson. *The Silence [of] Adam: Becoming Men of Courage in a World of Chaos.* Grand Rapids, Mich.: Zondervan Pub. House, 1995.

QUESTIONS

1. Have you fallen back into old habits or have you progressed a step?

2. Does your life reflect a biblical worldview or a worldly one (reference 1 John 2:15-17)?

3. Is money driving your life?

4. In your struggle against sin have you "stopped" habitual sin or does it still have victory over you?

5. What would happen if you lost everything—would you understand this as something for God to handle or would you try to handle it?

In this stage we may continue to struggle with these issues but are leaning more toward a biblical worldview, understanding God is in control and, while we have choices to make, it is God's plans that we *want to prevail.*

Stage Four—Ministry Development and Testing

Stage principles: Ministry discernment (where to get involved and where not to get involved) and testing of faith.

Minimum Time: 8-10 years as a committed Christian.

Calling: Understand their specific call at this stage and following that call.

Sin: Tempted back to old habits. Challenged by complacency and being lukewarm. Getting comfortable.

Max. percent living in flesh: 30%

Physical counter: Young adult—self-centered to other-centered.

+ / - Behavior: Pride. Humility. Complacency. Boldness.

Supporting Scriptures: Philippians 1:9-11, 1 Corinthians 3:6-9, Jeremiah 29:11.

Prominent Scripture: *To become perfect and mature, lacking nothing, we must have patience* (James 1:4).

MINISTRY DEVELOPMENT

Once we have repented of our bad behavior, have been baptized with Jesus, and are enlightened by Him, we get further involved in His business. We have not yet graduated from high school, but this is the last stage before we decide whether or not we go off to college. Since God's business was (and is) about love, we start to connect with other people's problems. The parable of the Good Samaritan (Luke 10:25-37) suggests we should stop our busy life to help someone in need, which we do, although we still may question the best way to do so. We don't just talk the talk, we start to walk the walk at a deeper level. When Jesus washed the disciples' feet, He made it clear that loving people was connected to serving them. In fact, as we get involved in Jesus' work, we become servants—just like He was (Philippians 2:1-8).

PETER

Jesus also made it clear what it meant to serve Him and to love Him in His instructions to Peter in John 21:15-19. He was very specific about our role as disciples, telling Peter to feed His lambs, and care for and feed His sheep. Jesus' instructions to Peter were about being a shepherd to God's people. This includes the poor, the homeless, those in prison, widows, orphans, and the like. As followers of Jesus Christ, this is what we will be judged on (see Matthew 25:31-46). We find it uncomfortable sitting on the sidelines as armchair quarterbacks regarding the work of God and His kingdom; we feel called to be in the game. We look for opportunities to "join God where He is already at work" (as Henry Blackaby would say), and we join Him. I checked myself into a homeless shelter at this stage in my own journey. Then I resigned from the church and accepted a job at the shelter because I felt called to serve Jesus by loving His poor. I wasn't completely sure what that meant, but, at this stage, I had to follow the whisper I heard from God in my heart.

TESTING

Unless our faith is tested, it is in question. Years ago, I went on a three-week trip to the Dominican Republic (DR). It was spiritual boot camp for me. Besides being very hot, I was the only Caucasian in the community where I was taken. There was no electricity, no running water, no bathrooms, no familiar food, and nobody spoke English. Then I got the flu. To say I was uncomfortable would be an understatement. The first night I was there they forgot about me so I slept in a very uncomfortable chair. The next night they gave me a bed with a bucket beside it in case I had to go to the bathroom during the night since they didn't have bathrooms. While I recognized the blessing of my new circumstances, I was way out of my comfort zone. Relief came a week later when a group of my friends came down as part of the mission trip I was coleading.

> So do not throw away this confident trust in the Lord. Remember the great reward it brings you! Patient endurance is what you need now, so that you will continue to do God's will. Then you will receive all that he has promised (Hebrews 10:32-36 NLT).

ETHIOPIA

I was tested another time in Ethiopia. We were offered the chance to go minister to the Hamar tribe, one of the most remote groups in the world. We were told they had been cannibals a couple of years prior to our visit. As it was verging on the rainy season, we were warned that if we got caught in one of the typical rains during the rainy season, we might not make it back without being airlifted out. Translated, we would be there for a lot longer than any of us had planned. Just like in the DR there was no electricity, no running water, no bathrooms, and no other Caucasians (except this time I was part of a team). We were warned that this trip was dangerous. We agreed to go. When we arrived, the tribesmen were dressed in rifles. Just rifles. Clothing was optional. Since they had not seen white people before or acted that way, they immediately started touching our hair and skin. Once again, I found myself in a very uncomfortable place. I was asked to speak using a translator, and was later told I was the first white man to share the gospel with this tribe. God honored the test.

> Consider it all joy, my brethren, when you encounter various trials, knowing that the testing of your faith produces endurance. And let endurance have *its* perfect result, so that you may be perfect and complete, lacking in nothing (James 1:2-4).

QUESTIONS

1. Are you actively involved in full-time ministry work as you pursue the calling God has on your life? This doesn't mean you are on staff at a church, or a missionary in some distant land, or even at an organization whose purpose is "ministry"—not at all (although you might be). Wherever you find yourself working—whatever job you have, do you realize you are in full-time ministry work and the purpose for the work you do is to minister to those around you by being Christlike toward them?

2. Are you really discipling others—pouring your life into a handful of other people?

3. Is your ministry life compartmentalized or whole? Do you intentionally include Christ in every facet of your life or do you "leave Him out" of some activities?

4. Do you realize the souls of those whose path you cross is at stake and that you play a part?

5. Do you help the less fortunate who you see or come across? Or is the work you do for yourself and ministry is something you do on weekends or when you show up to a small group meeting? Are the poor someone else's problem?

6. Are you maturing in your level of love for others and therefore seeing an increase in the patience you have for people—all people?

You are being tested in this stage—to find out what you truly believe you are doing on this earth. You cannot be struggling with habitual sin at this stage. If you realize you are in full-time ministry in this stage and your life reflects it—this may be the right stage.

Stage Five—Further Testing: Learning to Depend on Christ

Stage principles: Increased discernment, further testing, revelation of blind spots.

Minimum Time: 10-12 years as a committed Christians

Calling: Death of a vision. Wilderness experience. Resurrection of calling. Restoration.

Sin: Pride. Cynicism.

Max. percent living in flesh: 20% (this is a well disciplined person)

Physical counter: Adult. Able to disciple.

+ / - Behavior: Patience. Humility. Disciplined.

Supporting Scriptures: Jonah 2:8, Hebrews 12:5-7, 1 Peter 4:12-14.

Prominent Scripture: *These trials will show that your faith is genuine. It is being tested as fire tests and purifies gold—though your faith is far more precious than mere gold. So when your faith remains strong through many trials, it will bring you much praise and glory and honor on the day when Jesus Christ is revealed to the whole world* (1 Peter 1:6-7).

*"Slow down and enjoy life. It's not only the scenery you miss by going too fast—
you also miss the sense of where you are going and why."*
—Eddie Cantor

KNOW THYSELF

This stage is like moving from high school to college. You have a strong sense
of calling, might actually be living it, but your vision and mission are being
tested. You come face-to-face with the reality of your own faith through challenges in your life. This stage may include the disciple seeking affirmation of
their calling by spiritual leaders. Disciples going from stage four to stage five
should also have an accurate knowledge of their strengths and weaknesses
(limitations). A danger of moving to this stage is doing so without an accurate and realistic assessment of strengths and weaknesses by a mentor or wise
friend. I recently read a chapter in the book *Inside Job* that emphasized this
point. The author, Steve Smith, asks the reader to ask people these questions
in an effort to know thyself better: "What is it like to work for me? What is it
like to be on a team with me? What is it like to be my spouse? What is it like
to be my child?"[48] Those are hard questions to ask of those we care about or
care for, but they are worth asking in order that we don't over- or underesti-
mate our value to those around us. We may still live by the standards of the
flesh in some areas of our lives in this stage, *but we know it* and continue to
see progress in limiting the power our flesh has overall.

ADVANCED TESTING

According to the book of Job, God tests us often; these are advanced tests.[49]
One of the greatest tests of my life was when I moved into the urban area
of Charlotte. My comfortable, safe and peaceful life in South Charlotte was
replaced with regular gunfire in the distance, high crime, and roommates
who were addicted to drugs and mentally ill. And I was not on a short-term
mission trip. This was my new life. One night, after a very stressful day,
I was watching the few channels I could see on my small television, and
came across what appeared to be a documentary. It caught my eye. As I
watched this organization in New York City deal with folks with problems,
I started to notice similarities with my own housemates. Many of the folks
they were helping were homeless. It was as difficult an environment as I

48. Smith, Stephen W. *Inside Job: Doing the Work Within the Work.* Downer's Grove, Illinois: InterVarsity Press, 2015. 49.
49. See Job 7:18.

was dealing with. I actually laughed at the plight of their leaders because it was my trouble too! After about fifteen minutes, they described their organization as one helping the mentally ill. I had accepted a calling to help some of God's most challenged people. It would test my faith to an even greater level than other tests because I was called to live there! In doing so, most of my valuable possessions were stolen or ruined. It cost me my life—all of it.

The Bible says:

> Friends, when life gets really difficult, don't jump to the conclusion that God isn't on the job. Instead, be glad that you are in the very thick of what Christ experienced. This is a spiritual refining process, with glory just around the corner. If you're abused because of Christ, count yourself fortunate. It's the Spirit of God and his glory in you that brought you to the notice of others. If they're on you because you broke the law or disturbed the peace, that's a different matter. But if it's because you're a Christian, don't give it a second thought. Be proud of the distinguished status reflected in that name! (1 Peter 4:12-16 MSG)

Let's remember some biblical examples here: Abraham, the founder of our faith, was asked to sacrifice His only son, Isaac, as a test. Moses waited forty years before he was ready to deliver the Israelites; David waited ten years before he took over the throne from Saul; Paul spent many years being trained for his assignment; the disciples all fled from Jesus before fulfilling their callings as apostles; and Jesus was tested in the wilderness for forty days by Satan before He was led to the cross. And finally, let's not forget about Job. Stage five is about testing. When we pass the test, we move on to the next stage.

QUESTIONS

1. Has your love for others increased to the point your love is constantly in action? Do people know you as a disciple by the way you love others (John 13:35)?

2. Have you been through some recent and tough trials in your life?

3. How did you do in those trials?

4. Did you revert to a worldly response, trying to assume control, beating yourself up and others around you, as you tried to work your way out of the situation(s)?

5. Or did you let God handle them while you simply pressed in further to your heavenly Father, spending even more time in prayer and Bible reading, trusting Him to get you through?

If you let God handle your trials while you pressed into your heavenly Father, you are on your way to the next stage. If you chose to turn to an idol, you may be stuck. Turn your trials back over to God, remember you are His child, that He has a plan for your life and let Him do as He pleases with you. That is the faith that this stage requires. His grace will meet you there.

Stage Six—Ministry in the Power of Christ: Advanced Refinement, More Testing & Deeper Dependence on God

C.S. Lewis said, "Pain is God's megaphone."

Stage principles: Advanced refinement, testing and dependence.

Minimum Time: 12-14 years as a born-again Christian.

Calling: The disciple is focused on their calling, has been affirmed by someone with spiritual discernment (a nonmember of the family), and endures tests in a godly manner.

Sin: Disciple understands they are the worst of sinners because, like Paul, they are finally comparing themselves against God, not man. If the comparison were against man, this person is living a righteous life.

Max. percent living in flesh: 15%

Physical counter: Parent. Intentional disciplers.

+ / - Behavior: Balanced, steady, consistent and godly behavior.

Supporting Scriptures: Philippians 1:6, Romans 8:28, 1 Corinthians 2:3, 2 Corinthians 1:8-9. Until the time came to fulfill his dreams, the Lord tested Joseph's character (Psalm 105:19 NLT).

Prominent Scripture: *Then Jesus was led by the Spirit into the wilderness to be tempted by the devil. After fasting forty days and forty nights, he was hungry* (Matthew 4:1-2). Also a continuation of 1 Peter 1:6-7.

FURTHER TESTING AND GREATER FOCUS ON CHRISTIAN DISCIPLINES

The difference between stages five and six is how we handle our tests, not whether we have them or to what extent we have them. Our attitudes while being tested will reflect just how much we trust God despite our circumstances. Our prayer life at this stage should not require anyone reminding us or telling us how much we have to pray or why. We just do what it takes, knowing it is the most important thing we do. The same is true for studying the Word. It is our passion. We don't need any more convincing; we do it because we want to hear from God more than anything in the world. Fasting is not something we talk about either; we do it. This sets us up for stage seven. We have a tested eternal perspective. That does not mean we are fully mature, just well on the way. We depend on God's Spirit to sustain us to our greatest degree yet:

> We think you ought to know, dear brothers and sisters, about the trouble we went through in the province of Asia. We were crushed and overwhelmed beyond our ability to endure, and we thought we would never live through it. In fact, we expected to die. But as a result, we stopped relying on ourselves and learned to rely only on God, who raises the dead (2 Corinthians 1:8-9).

QUESTIONS

1. Do you consider yourself to be a disciplined soldier?

2. Have you been working decades in a calling that has been affirmed by other mature Christians and that is producing obvious fruit?

3. Does your behavior reflect the majority of the fruit of the spirit the majority of the time? (See Galatians 5:22,23.)

4. Are you balanced?

5. Are your priorities in order?

6. Have you let go of your right to be "right"?

7. Have you let go of a worldly definition of success for your ministry?

8. Are you becoming a pencil in the hand of God?

9. Do you realize you are a soldier in a full-blown spiritual war?

10. Do you thirst for God?

If you answered yes to those questions this appears to be your stage! If not, maybe this is a stage to shoot for.

Stage Seven—Maturity in Christ

Stage principles: Final engagement & maturity.

Minimum Time: 14-plus years as a born-again Christian.

Calling: Fully engaged in calling.

Sin: Fully dependent on God's grace.

Max. percent living in flesh: 10%

Physical counter: Grandparent. Selfless.

+ / - Behavior: It's all about grace (gracious behavior).

Supporting Scriptures: John 15:4-5, Colossians 1:5-6.

Prominent Scripture: *I have not achieved it, but I focus on this one thing: Forgetting the past and looking forward to what lies ahead, I press on to reach the end of the race and receive the heavenly prize for which God, through Christ Jesus, is calling us* (Philippians 3:13-14).

It took me quite a long time to develop a voice, and now that I have it, I am not going to be silent. —Madeleine Albright

DOCTORATE OF FRUIT

Sticking with the educational metaphor, stage seven is the doctorate. A primary characteristic of a mature Christian is one who is filled with the Holy Spirit. The proof of this maturity is their ability to rest in the sufficiency of Christ through the Holy Spirit rather than trusting in their flesh. They are often very calm in the midst of uncertainty. That is the fruit of the Holy Spirit.

Remain in me, as I also remain in you. No branch can bear fruit by itself; it must remain in the vine. Neither can you bear fruit unless you remain in me. I am the vine; you are the branches. If you remain in me and I in you, you will bear much fruit; apart from me you can do nothing (John 15:4).

Fruit, therefore, is the biblical measurement of a Christian: Not in a works-oriented fashion but in a character development-oriented one. If you go to the gym and exercise every day, the fruit of your efforts will be better endurance and stronger muscles. If you are close to God, you will exhibit His characteristics. Businessman and writer Stephen Covey[50] tells us to begin with

---

50. Covey, Stephen R. *The 7 Habits of Highly Effective People: Powerful Lessons in Personal Change.* New York, N.Y.: Simon & Schuster, 1989.

the end in mind. It is a business strategy that many refer to as *vision* and it keeps people and organizations focused. What should be our fruit if we are truly in relationship with God? The Bible says:

> But the fruit of the Spirit is love, joy, peace, patience, kindness, goodness, faithfulness, gentleness and self-control (Galatians 5:22-23).

JESUS

When we have His Spirit, our fruit is not how *much* we produce, but *how we behave* whether producing anything or not (since that fruit is ultimately up to God). Here is a passage written by Paul that summarizes the fruit of the Spirit:

> We live in such a way that no one will stumble because of us, and no one will find fault with our ministry. In everything we do, we show that we are true ministers of God. We patiently endure troubles and hardships and calamities of every kind. We have been beaten, been put in prison, faced angry mobs, worked to exhaustion, endured sleepless nights, and gone without food. We prove ourselves by our purity, our understanding, our patience, our kindness, by the Holy Spirit within us, and by our sincere love. We faithfully preach the truth. God's power is working in us. We use the weapons of righteousness in the right hand for attack and the left hand for defense. We serve God whether people honor us or despise us, whether they slander us or praise us. We are honest, but they call us impostors. We are ignored, even though we are well-known. We live close to death, but we are still alive. We have been beaten, but we have not been killed. Our hearts ache, but we always have joy. We are poor, but we give spiritual riches to others. We own nothing, and yet we have everything. Oh, dear Corinthian friends! We have spoken honestly with you, and our hearts are open to you. There is no lack of love on our part, but you have withheld your love from us. I am asking you to respond as if you were my own children. Open your hearts to us! (2 Corinthians 6:3-13).

QUESTIONS

1. Are you dead yet?

I am not sure how many of us get to this stage too long before we pass to the other side of eternity, but one question you can ask yourself to truly understand if you are at this stage or not is whether you are dead yet—to this world. You love God above all else and are a full-time servant putting others needs ahead of your own. You understand what it means to love your enemies and you do. Rather than complain, you turn everything over to God. Your life is one of sacrifice and humility. Your flesh really does not count for anything (John 6:63). You are a pencil in the hand of God.

Congratulations if you were able to accurately assess yourself.

It may be beneficial for you to go back to the matrix at the beginning of the chapter and look over the stage in which you find yourself. Consider others in your life—perhaps those on staff at your church or your parachurch, your board of directors, your group leader, or your disciples. Based on what you know about them, what stage do you think they fit best? Do you know? If you do not know, get together with them and ask them some of the questions found throughout the stages. As stated, there is nothing absolute about this assessment, but it should wake us up to the reality that we need to assess one another for the sake of our army. We are our brother's keeper—particularly those who are in leadership:

> Has it ever dawned on you that you are responsible spiritually to God for other people? For instance, if I allow any turning away from God in my private life, everyone around me suffers. We "sit together in the heavenly places ..." (Ephesians 2:6 NKJV). "If one member suffers, all the members suffer with it ..." (1 Corinthians 12:26 NKJV). "If you allow physical selfishness, mental carelessness, moral insensitivity, or spiritual weakness, everyone in contact with you will suffer. But you ask, "Who is sufficient to be able to live up to such a lofty standard?" "Our sufficiency is from God ..." and God alone" (2 Corinthians 3:5 NKJV).[51]

Now let's look at a fair way of assessing the local church and parachurch organizations.

---

51. Chambers, Oswald. "Am I My Brother's Keeper?" My Utmost For His Highest. February 15, 2015. Accessed November 3, 2015.

CHAPTER 14
QUESTIONS

1. According to these stages, what stage are you in?

2. Who knows you well enough and is comfortable enough to talk to you that would affirm or challenge your answer in number one?

3. Even if you consider these to be inaccurate representations of the process a Christian goes through toward maturity, can you see a benefit in considering them?

4. Where else in someone's life can they get an important job without assessment?

5. Have you ever hired anyone? Did you assess them before hiring them? What information did you rely on to evaluate them?

15 Assessing Our Churches and Parachurches

"You don't climb mountains without a team, you don't climb mountains without being fit, you don't climb mountains without being prepared and you don't climb mountains without balancing the risks and rewards. And you never climb a mountain on accident—it has to be intentional."
—Mark Udall

HOW THE CHURCH'S DNA COMPARES TO OTHER ORGANIZATIONS

The second solution is implementing a process to assess our churches and parachurches. Rather than look at the typical criteria for assessment: how many attend church each weekend, the church budget, how many professions of faith have been made, how many are active in ministry, etc., I want to focus on what I have learned is the DNA of a healthy organization—any organization. This secular evaluation process centers on the health of the average small group of the organization being reviewed. Since the group model appears to be the 21st century model of the church, and where true discipleship is supposed to happen, it goes to follow that evaluating those groups would provide an appropriate assessment of our churches. We can do this by looking at two areas:

1. Optimal size of a group

2. Specific DNA of a healthy group

OPTIMAL SIZE TEAM

All the studies I found regarding optimal team size were in agreement: a healthy small group should have between five and twelve members. They cited sports as a point of reference. Football and soccer teams have eleven players; hockey has six; basketball has five; and baseball has nine. The sports model fits the optimal team size. *Fortune Magazine* did a study in business and found the optimal team size to be 4.6, although I am not sure how they got that number.[52] They also cited a study done in 1913 by Maximilien Ringelmann, called "The Ringelmann Theory" or "social loafing." Ringelmann, a French social psychologist and professor of agricultural engineering, studied whether the efforts of a group of individuals were greater than the sum total of the individuals in the group. To determine this he had individuals tug on a rope one at a time, then he had the entire group pull that same rope at the same time. His discovery? The sum total of all the individual exertion was greater than that of the group.

THE BIGGER THE GROUP, THE LESS EFFORT BY A GROUP MEMBER

People gave less effort when they were *hidden in a larger group*. That is why this theory is often referred to as social loafing; the larger the group, the easier it is for one person to hide or not have to exert as much effort as they would if they were alone.[53] This was confirmed by Wharton Management Professor Katherine Klein, who found that individuals can "free ride" in larger teams of greater than eight or nine people.[54] Based upon this information, let's agree that the optimal group size is less than or equal to 12 people. And let's remember that when we discuss the fact that Jesus had 12 disciples.

DNA OF A HEALTHY GROUP

Implied by this information is that large churches *can* disciple their body as well as their smaller counterparts, *if the teams in the organization are smaller and healthier.* That brings us to our second criteria, assessing the specific DNA of the average group.

According to Group Dynamics, the DNA of a healthy business can be understood by an assessment of its inherent groups. If the average group found in a business has the following characteristics, the business is likely healthy, regardless of its size:

• A shared purpose

• Clear goals

• Specific roles with competent team members

• A light and engaging atmosphere

52. Useem, Jerry. "Fortune." Secrets of Great Teams: How to Build a Great Team. May 31, 2006. Accessed October 1, 2015.
53. Wikipedia contributors. "Max Ringelmann." *Wikipedia, The Free Encyclopedia.* Accessed October 1, 2015.
54. Klein, Katherine. "Is Your Team Too Big? Too Small? What's the Right Number?—Knowledge@ Wharton." KnowledgeWharton Is Your Team Too Big Too Small What's the Right Number Comments. Accessed October 1, 2015.

- Mutual accountability and transparency
- Pursuit of excellence
- Continuous learning
- Passion, unity, and commitment[55]

Let's take a closer look at each of these characteristics. I have added Scripture where applicable to keep this discussion focused on our topic. I am also assuming a level of discernment over how critical one characteristic is over another for purposes of our small-group model in the church. Not everyone in a church small group may have a specific role the same way as its business counterpart or a group of staff members. Use your judgment to assess your own group accordingly.

SHARED PURPOSE, CLEAR GOALS, SPECIFIC ROLES

A purpose is greater than an intentional goal, but without both a purpose and a target, a group is not in focus. If you don't have focus, you have no foundation for your team. Can you imagine a sports team going into a game not knowing what they were supposed to do? Winning a championship doesn't always have to be the goal of a sports team. The team may have other goals, but there must be a goal for the team to aim for in order for it to reach its optimal level of success. Have an agreed-upon target.

So whether we are at home or away, we make it our aim to please him (2 Corinthians 5:9 ESV).

Roles are similarly important. Can you imagine the center of a football team getting on the field and deciding he wanted to be the quarterback instead because he felt like taking a shot at that position? Ridiculous, right? But, in some organizations, that is exactly what people do and how they think. The next chapter covers this issue of roles more specifically, but for now consider the leader of your group since that is the primary position for our small groups. Or if you are a group leader, consider your own competencies. Is your leader in the proper role? Do others in your group have roles as well?

ATMOSPHERE

The atmosphere of an organization (which includes its culture) is also important. The team needs to have an encouraging atmosphere that is not in contradiction to its people.

---

55. Mack, Coach. "What Is the DNA of an Effective Team? -." Group Dynamix RSS2. September 17, 2014. Accessed October 1, 2015.

Therefore encourage one another and build each other up, just as in fact you are doing (1 Thessalonians 5:11).

Creative people, for instance, don't do well on intense teams. They need to have flexibility to create and that typically means a less intense or lighter ambiance. Those dealing with finance or other issues need more attention to details and the time to do things right. Salespeople sometimes need a bit more push to get moving, thus the pressure associated with a sales quota. Your church small group will also have diversity. Your evangelists will be outgoing and like to talk. Your servants may be more reserved and not have much to say. The group atmosphere must be able to engage everyone, which might mean putting a lid on the evangelist and probing the servant. Just do it in an encouraging manner to keep a positive and energized atmosphere.

ACCOUNTABILITY

Accountability is critical as we know from our previous solution. It is built into both the sports and the education models, since both areas are competitive. Sports teams have games. Education has tests and grades. These models have been built by a system of evaluation. We need to do the same to the degree it keeps our group healthy:

1. Do you know the struggles of those in your group?

2. Have you heard their testimony—their raw testimony?

3. Have your members matured in their walk over the past several months?

4. Do you meet at times other than your group time?

5. Does your group help others in need, minister to the community, serve the poor?

Consider concrete areas to measure your group and then do so.

TRANSPARENCY

Transparency is another essential component of the group. The opposite of transparency is politics. Based upon my experiences, it is important to differentiate between the two. The definition of politics that I am using is the one that assumes one cannot share things honestly with others because they will not understand you, and *your comments will either become an obstacle to the outcome you want or they will be used against you later*. That definition of politics is self-focused for a greater good desired by the person engaging in politics. Transparency is being able to bring things that are in the darkness into the light without fear of judgment:

Therefore, there is now no condemnation for those who are in Christ Jesus (Romans 8:1).

If someone does not feel comfortable enough to say what they need to say, the group will suffer and become more "political" than transparent. It will never reach its full potential. A healthy group needs to have people in it who are willing to share because they trust the other members' ability to hear them, and keep confidential matters, confidential.

EXCELLENCE

A standard of excellence means one cares about the quality of work accomplished by the group. It also means the members of the group honor commitments. Group members show up on time, participate in group activities. The Bible says:

Whatever you do, work at it with all your heart, as working for the Lord, not for human masters (Colossians 3:23).

A healthy group needs to have a desire for excellence embedded in their DNA. A group that doesn't strive for excellence isn't a healthy group.

TRAINING

The faster information changes, the more important training becomes. Because of technology, information is changing at a faster rate today than at any time in history. Training is essential in our efforts to keep pace with the world. It is also imperative in our efforts to stay connected to the vine of Christ. The Bible says:

All Scripture is inspired by God and is useful to teach us what is true and to make us realize what is wrong in our lives. It corrects us when we are wrong and teaches us to do what is right. God uses it to prepare and equip his people to do every good work (2 Timothy 3:16-17 NLT).

The Bible also claims to be a lamp to our feet, a light to our path (Psalm 119:105). It is the living Word (Hebrews 4:12). It is where God speaks to His children. We should constantly study the Bible:

Keep this Book of the Law always on your lips; meditate on it day and night, so that you may be careful to do everything written in it. Then you will be prosperous and successful (Joshua 1:8).

PASSIONATE COMMITMENT

The final characteristic of a healthy group is passionate commitment. It is integral to have team members committed to the mission and vision of the group. This is more than just being committed for commitment's sake. If you are committed to quitting smoking, you will try hard not to smoke. But if you are passionate about being healthy and committed to quitting smoking for the sake of an extended life, feeling better, being able to run a marathon, or something more concrete than just quitting for quitting's sake, you will have a better chance at succeeding. Many of us focus on getting over our problem(s) without focusing on the benefits of doing so. When you are passionate about something and committed to it because of your passion, you will stay the course despite obstacles. If you are not, you probably won't. A healthy team requires people who are more passionate about what they are doing than their own bad habits.

As iron sharpens iron, so one person sharpens another (Proverbs 27:17).

Those are the characteristics of a healthy group.

ORGANIZATIONAL LID

Now let's apply this to your organization. On a scale of one to ten, one being the lowest grade and ten being the highest, rate the average small group of your church or parachurch using the following table. If you are a small-group leader or a participant in a group, rate your own group as well:

GROUP ASSESSMENT	EXPLANATION	1-10
Number of group members?	*Who is in your group? Are there more than 12?	
A shared purpose?	Do group members understand the purpose for the group? What is that purpose?	
Clear goals?	Are group members pursuing specific and measurable goals? Can you list those goals here?	

GROUP ASSESSMENT	EXPLANATION	1-10
Specific roles with competent team members?	Do group members have different roles in the group? If so, can you define them?	
A light and engaging atmosphere?	Do the group members feel comfortable sharing w/o someone trying to "fix" them? Do group members share deep hurts, wounds or struggles?	
Mutual accountability and transparency?	Is there God-centered but biblical accountability for behavior? How are you held accountable?	
Pursuit of excellence?	Is there a commitment to Christ and His work or is the group all about self? Does the group regularly "serve" together?	
Continuous learning?	Are group members committed to continued growth? How so?	
Passion, unity, and commitment?	Are group members committed to the group? How is this expressed? Does your group meet outside of group time?	

* If you have 12 or fewer people in your group, give yourself a score of 10.
Scoring:

0 – 60: Low impact. Unhealthy.
61 – 74: Medium impact. In between healthy and unhealthy.
75 – 90: High impact. Healthy.

Congratulations! You have now evaluated the man or woman in the mirror as well as the average group of your church or parachurch or of your own small group. Hopefully the group you assessed is healthy, high impact.

If not, if your group or the average group of your church or parachurch is not deemed to be healthy based upon this assessment, measures should be taken to develop your group or group model even if that means replacing leaders. John Maxwell refers to this as "the law of the leadership lid"[56]—an organization cannot rise above its leader or leadership team. I will refer to it as the law of the organization lid. No organization can rise beyond the health of its average group. This takes us to the next solution, assessing whether we have the right people in the right position in both our church or parachurch organizations.

---

56. "Leadership Wired Blog: The Law of the Lid." The John Maxwell Company. July 19, 2013. Accessed October 1, 2015.

CHAPTER 15
QUESTIONS

1. Have you ever been on a successful team or in a successful group? What made that experience successful?

2. Have you ever been on an unsuccessful team (or group)? Describe that experience.

3. If you have a favorite sports team, do you know why they might be successful or unsuccessful based upon the information provided in this chapter?

4. Still apprehensive about the issue of assessment? If you discovered the restaurant you were about to eat at was given a poor rating by the health inspector, would you still eat at that restaurant?

16 Ensuring the Right People Are in the Right Jobs

"Leaders of companies that go from good to great start not with 'where' but with 'who.' They start by getting the right people on the bus, the wrong people off the bus, and the right people in the right seats."[57]
—Jim Collins

Now that we have an assessment process for our congregants and for our church group model, we need to ensure we are putting our most qualified people into leadership positions. This is our third solution.

SCALE

Diagram 4 (page 151) illustrates the connection between stages of discipleship and job categories. I do not believe we should start hiring based upon the perfect resume, interview, background, or behavior, but I think we need to consider which stage of discipleship a person is at before giving them a position in our churches or parachurch organizations that they may not be able to handle. As Henry Blackaby teaches in *Experiencing God*, God develops our character to match our assignment.[58] Let's also remember:

> From everyone who has been given much, much will be demanded; and from the one who has been entrusted with much, much more will be asked (Luke 12:48). Not many of you should become teachers, my fellow believers, because you know that we who teach will be judged more strictly (James 3:1).

And to reiterate, I have already said candidates *must meet regularly* in a small group of committed peers where they are accountable for their behavior and growth.

57. Collins, Jim. "Good to Great." Article. October 2001. Accessed November 20, 2015.
58. Blackaby, Henry T., and Claude V. King. *Experiencing God: How to Live the Full Adventure of Knowing and Doing the Will of God*. Nashville, Tenn.: Broadman & Holman Publishers, 1994. Unit 2, page 46.

MEASUREMENT

As noted, we are measuring Christians based upon the following criteria:

1. Time: How long has it been since they have made a commitment to Christ?

2. Calling: How well do they understand their calling?

3. Personal behavior: How well does the behavior of this person line up with proper biblical behavior?

4. Experience: How much experience do they have in their calling?

DUTIES AND STATES

For entry-level positions including administrative duties, maintenance, and other non-leadership or non-supervisory positions, the Christian seeking employment need only be a stage one or two disciple. Someone who has made a commitment to Christ as their Lord and Savior and is growing in their relationship can adequately handle an entry-level position in a Christian organization. However, and let me be clear, putting a non-Christian into a Christian organization can and will have an impact on the organization. It opens the door for more and more folks to enter the organization without Jesus. In the beginning this may not matter at all. But oftentimes what starts out innocently enough (as outreach) ends up as transformation of an organization into something it was never intended to be: lukewarm or agnostic. The Bible tells us not to yoke ourselves with nonbelievers for a reason:

> Do not be yoked together with unbelievers. For what do righteousness and wickedness have in common? Or what fellowship can light have with darkness? (2 Corinthians 6:14).

Internships, residencies, or entry-level supervisory positions should be at a discipleship stage of three or four. These folks are *overseers* and need to be at a maturity level that allows them to be examples to less-mature Christians. The same is true for our small group leaders. They should not be struggling with a toxic addiction and should have several years knowing and following Christ with a good track record:

> He must not be a recent convert, or he may become conceited and fall under the same judgment as the devil (1 Timothy 3:6).

DIAGRAM 4

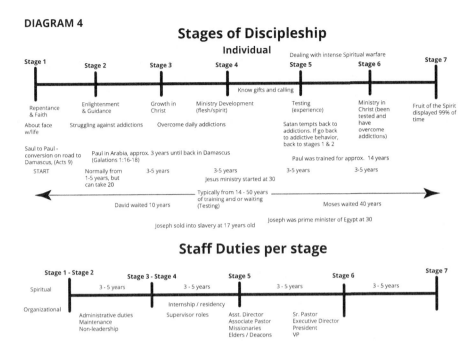

Stages of Discipleship

Individual

Dealing with intense Spiritual warfare

Stage 1	Stage 2	Stage 3	Stage 4	Stage 5	Stage 6	Stage 7

Know gifts and calling

Repentance & Faith	Enlightenment & Guidance	Growth in Christ	Ministry Development (flesh/spirit)	Testing (experience)	Ministry in Christ (been tested and	Fruit of the Spirit displayed 99% of time
About face w/life	Struggling against addictions	Overcome daily addictions		Satan tempts back to addictions. If go back to addictive behavior, back to stages 1 & 2	have overcome addictions)	

Saul to Paul - conversion on road to Damascus, (Acts 9)

Paul in Arabia, approx. 3 years until back in Damascus (Galations 1:16-18)

Paul was trained for approx. 14 years

| START | Normally from 1-5 years, but can take 20 | 3-5 years | 3-5 years Jesus ministry started at 30 | 3-5 years | 3-5 years | |

Typically from 14 - 50 years of training and or waiting (Testing)

David waited 10 years

Moses waited 40 years

Joseph was prime minister of Egypt at 30

Joseph sold into slavery at 17 years old

Staff Duties per stage

Stage 1 - Stage 2	Stage 3 - Stage 4	Stage 5	Stage 6	Stage 7
Spiritual	3 - 5 years	3 - 5 years	3 - 5 years	3 - 5 years

Organizational

Internship / residency

	Administrative duties Maintenance Non-leadership	Supervisor roles	Asst. Director Associate Pastor Missionaries Elders / Deacons	Sr. Pastor Executive Director President VP

Of course this does not mean this applicant is without sin. It implies that habitual sin is behind the disciple. Elders, deacons, assistant directors, associate pastors, or even missionaries should be at or above stage five in the discipleship process. Pastors, executive directors, presidents, vice presidents, and anyone running an organization should have at least reached stage five and be well toward stage six. Remember, if we are using the education model as a parallel: stage five is college, six is graduate school, and seven is a doctorate. There are always exceptions to rules like this, but I would be very careful before breaking them. Education is not a panacea, but it has its place, just like these stages of discipleship.

GODLY BEHAVIOR

High impact senior-level positions, our most gifted leaders, should be filled with people who exhibit the fruit of the Spirit to a formidable degree. What qualifies a person for spiritual leadership at this level is *godly character*—and godly character established according to the clear criteria found in 1 Timothy 3:

Blameless, the husband of one wife, temperate, sober-minded, of good behavior, hospitable, able to teach; not given to wine, not violent, not greedy for money, but gentle, not quarrelsome, not covetous; one who rules his own house well, having *his* children in submission with all reverence (for if a man does not know how to rule his own house, how will he take care of the church of God?); not a novice, lest being puffed up with pride he fall into the *same* condemnation as the devil. Moreover he must have a good testimony among those who are outside, lest he fall into reproach and the snare of the devil (1 Timothy 3:1-7 NKJV).

Parachurch organizations that put non-Christians or baby Christians into *leadership positions in their Christian organization,* thinking they are still a strong Christian organization, are in for trouble:

If anyone shows up who doesn't hold to this teaching, don't invite him in and give him the run of the place. That would just give him a platform to perpetuate his evil ways, making you his partner (2 John 10-11 The Message).

I hate to rock the boat, but a tidal wave is going to hit those boats if they are not rocked back into proper order first. Let us remember:

It wasn't raining when Noah built the ark. —Howard Ruff

Any organization that is not built on the foundation of Christ is eventually going to meet a storm that it cannot withstand. Satan does not play fair. Like I said, everything catches up to us eventually. We must implement biblical boundaries in our Christian organizations. But we also must remember that God uses whatever choices we make for our good and His glory, as believers, even if they appear wrong or unsuccessful from our limited perspective (Romans 8:28). Jesus chose Judas. That should give us a sense of peace that we cannot fail as long as we trust God in the midst of any apparent failure and don't give up. On the other hand, it should not eliminate our desire to follow biblical guidelines for leaders and do our best to put the right person in the right position (Colossians 3:23).

We also need a process of recovery for Christian soldiers caught up in this spiritual war. That is our next solution.

CHAPTER 16
QUESTIONS

1. Based upon your current stage, what job (or leadership position) should you have in a church or parachurch organization?

2. What job (or leadership position) do you have, if you are working in a church or parachurch?

3. What will you do with any discrepancy between your stage and the job you have?

4. Are you willing to be accountable to a higher stage?

5. Are you a good candidate for hire by another organization? If so, why should someone hire you?

17 Not Shooting Our Soldiers When They're Wounded

"Dear brothers and sisters, if another believer is overcome by some sin, you who are godly should gently and humbly help that person back onto the right path. And be careful not to fall into the same temptation yourself. Share each other's burdens, and in this way obey the law of Christ. If you think you are too important to help someone, you are only fooling yourself. You are not that important."
—Galatians 6:1-3

The fourth solution is dealing with our disciples in a biblical manner—particularly when they fall. This solution is about our need to stop shooting wounded soldiers when they are caught in sin, and help them on their road to recovery instead. This is where this book's title intersects with reality. Oftentimes we seek to fire someone before we ever understand the role we are supposed to play in his or her life. It is therefore worthy of a discussion.

SPIRITUAL POLLUTION

The leading cause of death in China is cancer. Only 1% of the 560 million inhabitants who live in cities breathe air that is considered safe. China often appears covered with a toxic gray cloud. Their air is polluted. Many people are dying as a result, and others have to change the way they live in order to deal with the pollution. If you are a runner in the United States who is used to going outside to take a daily run, you would likely suffer lung problems if you ran in China. Pollution is bad for the health of a body. It is the same spiritually. If a person is polluted by the world, it means being overcome by sin. The Bible tells us we are not to become polluted by the world, which implies being tangled up in sin. According to John Piper, sin is:

"The glory of God not honored. The holiness of God not reverenced. The greatness of God not admired. The power of God not praised. The truth of God not sought. The wisdom of God not esteemed. The beauty of God not treasured. The goodness of God not savored. The faithfulness of God not

trusted. The commandments of God not obeyed. The justice of God not respected. The wrath of God not feared. The grace of God not cherished. The presence of God not prized. The person of God not loved. That is sin."[59]

There are over 700 behaviors identified as *sin* in the Bible. Even though we live in an incredibly self-absorbed culture that condones same-sex marriage, change of gender, abortion, and greed, this should not be the case in our lives. Believers cannot continue in sin. Followers of Christ experience a changed life—it comes with the territory.

No one who abides in him keeps on sinning; no one who keeps on sinning has either seen him or known him (1 John 3:6).

But we must deal with sin in a biblical manner.

STONE THE SINNER

There are two extremes in the church regarding sin. On the one hand there are those who want to stone the sinner at the first sign of sin by becoming part of the mob. This group was called the Pharisees in the Bible. They were the holier-than-thou crowd of Jesus' day. Jesus challenged the Pharisees thus:

When they kept on questioning him, he straightened up and said to them, "Let any one of you who is without sin be the first to throw a stone at her" (John 8:7).

People who think they need to stone someone for their behavior need to be careful about their level of judgment. We must first assess our own lives before we begin to speak into another person's life:

You hypocrite, first take the plank out of your own eye, and then you will see clearly to remove the speck from your brother's eye (Matthew 7:5).

We will be judged the way we judge others so this is very important to all of us:

For in the same way you judge others, you will be judged, and with the measure you use, it will be measured to you (Matthew 7:2).

---

59. Piper, John. *Desiring God: Meditations of a Christian Hedonist*. Colorado Springs, Colo.: Multnomah, 2011.

SLOPPY AGAPE

On the other hand, there are those who think that God is so kind, that their sin does not matter. Regardless of how long or how often they struggle with their sin, everything will be OK. They are doing all right. Pastor David Chadwick calls that belief *sloppy agape*. It's a misunderstanding of God's grace. And the Bible agrees:

> You didn't think, did you, that just by pointing your finger at others you would distract God from seeing all your misdoings and from coming down on you hard? Or did you think that because he's such a nice God, he'd let you off the hook? Better think this one through from the beginning. God is kind, but he's not soft. In kindness he takes us firmly by the hand and leads us into a radical life change (Romans 2:3-4 MSG).

Sloppy agape is when we hide under grace instead of quitting our sinful behavior. That does not mean we are forced to be perfect, as some will argue when pressed. Everybody knows that none of us is perfect; all of us struggle with something. But we are not supposed to be a slave to our sin:

> For a man is enslaved to whatever has mastered him (2 Peter 2:19).

RICH YOUNG RULER

I think the best example of this is the rich young ruler. This man approaches Jesus to find out what he has to do to receive eternal life. It is a great question. But Jesus knows the man's heart. He knows what he is clinging to and won't give up, so He tells him to do just that!

> Just then a man came up to Jesus and asked, "Teacher, what good thing must I do to get eternal life?" "Why do you ask me about what is good?" Jesus replied. "There is only One who is good. If you want to enter life, keep the commandments. "Which ones?" he inquired. Jesus replied, "You shall not murder, you shall not commit adultery, you shall not steal, you shall not give false testimony, honor your father and mother,' and 'love your neighbor as yourself.' "All these I have kept," the young man said. "What do I still lack?" Jesus answered, "If you want to be perfect, go, sell your possessions and give to the poor, and you will have treasure in heaven. Then come, follow me." When the young man heard this, he went away sad, because he had great wealth (Matthew 19:16-22).

In a culture that despises absolutes, Jesus was absolutely clear in His response to the rich man. God will always point out the areas of struggle we have in our life. While we may brag about the areas in our life that we have overcome, God is not asking us to have partial obedience to Him; He wants us to overcome all things that hinder us. Let's just call it what it is—idolatry. Jesus asked the rich man to sell all his possessions because He knew the man's money was his god. God wants us to overcome each and every obstacle through His Holy Spirit in us. That's His plan, but like any plan, there are steps that must be taken to get the best results. Anyone who does not have an accountability partner and who is not in a small group of Christians focused on growing in their relationship with Christ is at risk to the evil one. No exceptions. If you are not in a small group and are not held accountable to biblical behavior—it is likely your calling has already been negatively impacted. As for those struggling against sin: What do we do when they fall? How do we help one another pick up the pieces when things fall apart? Let me use Hoskins Park Ministries as a possible template.

A RESCUE PLAN, OR STARTING OVER WELL

At Hoskins Park, we developed a twelve-month recovery plan to help those who were constantly falling into sin. A sample of it is represented in the following graph. The first three months for any staff member are considered probationary, under review. The staff member is not allowed to have any supervisory role. Given successful completion of the recovery plan, the next phase allows for some supervision while the staff member continues to participate in the program. After six successful months in the recovery process, the staff member can return to a supervisory role; after nine to twelve months, the staff member can return to his position, given successful completion of the counseling, a working Life Transformation Plan (LTP), and an accountability partner. The caveat here is that there is no debate over the definition of sin. As I get to later, I was stunned to learn that some Christians think sin is up to someone's individual conviction. It is not. Struggling against sin is one thing; accepting sin as okay is a totally different issue.

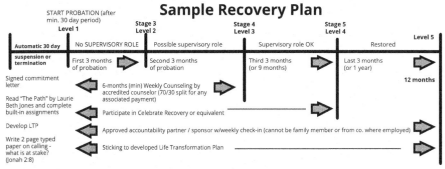

Sample Recovery Plan

The Life Transformation Plan (LTP) and 2 page typed paper must be approved by Board of Directors of HPM.

The counselor, CR or Equiv., and accountability partner must be approved by Board of Directors of HPM.

While in the recovery process, if there is any non-approved deviation from this plan, or another relapse, or any behavior that the board of directors of Hoskins Park Ministries deems unsuitable to the ministry, the probationary employee will be terminated and start the cycle over again with one month added to the suspension/termination for each subsequent relapse.

Church or biblical discipline

When someone is dealing with sin, whether unintentional or not, here are the biblical steps that need to be followed:

Matthew 18:15-17

• Confront person and mention the issue in private.
• If he or she does not listen, go with one or two others.
• If he or she still refuses to listen, take the matter before the church or body.

• If still no repentance, remove person from establishment (1 Corinthians 5:2-13)
• Once person repents, forgive and comfort (2 Corinthians 2:5-8)
• If disobedient, do not associate (2 Thessalonians 3:14-15).
• After two warnings, still no response, reject person (Titus 3:10).

RECOVERY

The Life Transformation Plan includes information obtained from The Ex-changed Life of Grace Life International out of Charlotte, NC.[60] It takes the fallen soldier through past hurts, habits, and hang-ups. This is from First United Methodist Church of Mansfield:[61]

Hurt—To experience physical pain caused by yourself or another; to feel emotional pain; undergo or experience difficulties or setbacks. The feeling of being hurt is an emotional reaction to another person's behavior or to a disturbing situation (e.g., abuse, abandonment, codependency, divorce, relationship issues, etc.).

Hang-up—A psychological or emotional problem or fixation about something. An issue that causes persistent impediment or source of delay. Hang-ups are negative mental attitudes that are used to cope with people or adversity (e.g., anger, depression, fear, un-forgiveness, etc.).

---

60. Used by permission, Grace Life International, 1337 Hundred Oaks Drive, Charlotte, NC, 28217.
61. The Landing, First United Methodist Church of Mansfield, Amanda Hardeman, pdf, Hurts———Habits———and———Hang-Ups. Accessed October 15, 2015.

Habit—Regular, repeated behavior pattern. An action or pattern of behavior that is repeated so often that it becomes typical of somebody, although he or she may be unaware of it. Addiction, such as an addiction to a drug, food, or some other stimuli that deadens ones feelings. A habit is an addiction to someone or something (e.g., alcohol dependency, drugs, food, gambling, sex, shopping, smoking, etc.).

The Life Transformation Plan includes understanding the issue of grace as it intersects with our past, godly targets, tactics, and strategies to accomplish specific goals. For someone struggling, we also suggest counseling for a minimum of six months with a Christian organization (such as Grace Life) or attendance at AA or Celebrate Recovery, a Christian 12-step plan for addiction. If the staff member complies with all this in twelve months, he or she is given back his or her job. If they are unable to comply, we are unable to help them further.

CASE STUDY: HOSKINS PARK

In the case of Hoskins Park, one of the staff used crack again. The person was not terminated. HPM staff worked with her, discerning her progress (or lack thereof), until she used again and was dismissed. Another employee refused to participate in the program and left the organization. He has returned as a participant in the ministry, but has no staff authority. While the recovery we have put together is certainly not a panacea, it does help us maintain a discipleship program without shooting our wounded. It also reminds us how much time just one person takes to disciple.

CHAPTER 17
QUESTIONS

1. If your child was found using drugs, at what point would you kick them out of your house: Using one time? Two times? Three times? Never? When is enough, enough for your child?

2. How is your child different than someone else's child who you do not know well?

3. When is enough enough for a homeless person to continue in their addiction?

4. Knowing we are all sinners in need of a Savior, where would you draw the line regarding the following situations: Two people of the opposite sex living together without being married? Someone involved in pornography? Someone who is obese? A smoker? A liar? An adulterer?

5. How do Jesus' words "let he who is without sin throw the first stone" impact your thoughts?

6. Has anything you have read up to this point changed your previously held views about your answers? If so, how?

18 Discipleship Requires Time—Do We Have Enough?

"It's one thing to believe in sacrifice, it's another to live with it."
—Unknown

Solution number five is the recognition that the kind of discipleship required for our light to transform the darkness requires more time and sacrifice than we might want to give or think we have.

HARVESTING CROPS

We have addressed the different stages of discipleship, our target, and the issue of recovery as a component of discipleship. I want to put this into practical terms. Richard Stearns compares the discipleship process to harvesting crops.[62] Someone has to prepare the land. If there are trees, roots, rocks, etc. on the land, they must be removed. The soil needs to be broken up and prepared with fertilizer before the seeds are even planted. Then the seeds must be nurtured through obstacles such as nasty weather, hungry animals and insects, and even manmade disasters. If you have ever done any work on a farm, you understand how difficult all of those steps are. Nothing about that process is easy. I have a personal story that illustrates my own view—my first Ironman Triathlon. An Ironman is a 2.4-mile swim, followed by a 112-mile bike ride, followed by a 26.2-mile run. This story is a strong reflection of the problems we face in our discipleship process. It might sound like an extreme example of discipleship by some. But what if this is supposed to be the norm—at least for a few of our disciples?

THE IRONMAN TRIATHLON

When I was in my mid-twenties, I stood on the sidelines in Kona, Hawaii, and watched some of the participants of the Ironman Triathlon run by. I worked for Apple and just happened to be there for the Apple Worldwide Sales Conference. I thought these athletes were out of their minds. Having

62. Stearns, Richard. *A Hole In Our Gospel: What Does God Expect of Us? The Answer That Changed My Life and Might Just Change the World.* Nashville, TN: Thomas Nelson, 2009. 7.

completed a sprint triathlon, I knew how challenging that had been for me at a fraction of those distances. The idea of completing a full Ironman was out of the question. I wouldn't, I couldn't. It was impossible for me. Then I married Kate, a triathlete. We watched an episode of *The Biggest Loser* which featured one of the winners successfully completing a half Ironman. One of Kate's dreams was to do a full Ironman. We decided if that contestant could lose all that weight and complete a half Ironman, we could do a full one. Kate's goal became mine as I started to believe I could do an Ironman myself, even though it was twenty years after thinking it was impossible. That became our target, our goal. We signed up to do the Ironman in Coeur d'Alene, Idaho.

TRAINING

In order to complete this formidable feat and reach our goal, we had to make drastic life changes. These were my top three:

1. First, I had to be converted from a night owl to a morning person— something that was not easy for me to do. For the eight months prior to the race, we were regularly up at four-something in the morning to exercise. That was drastic change number one.

2. Second, we had to exercise a lot, a whole lot! That meant riding our bikes in sub-freezing temperatures before the sun was shining, running more miles than I care to recall—sometimes right after getting off our bikes—and swimming. We also had to include a daily stretching routine and weight training to keep our muscles strong enough to endure the long distances. This was drastic change number two.

3. Third, my diet had to change. We had to keep sweets to a minimum in order to avoid cramps and focus on proper nutrition to endure the training. You can have a well-trained body and still not complete an Ironman because of a lack of proper nutrition. As a struggling sugar addict, this was the third and final drastic change. I gave up sodas completely in order to achieve this goal.

FINAL PREPARATION

We hired a part-time coach who let us know how much to train, gave us tips on nutrition, and encouraged our progress. We also found training guides online and researched advice from experienced Ironman participants. Then, coincidentally, I was asked to speak at a Rotary Club meeting nearby. During my talk on the subject of love, I mentioned the upcoming race and said success would be defined not by how I did personally, but by how my wife did. As her husband, I took it as my responsibility to help her achieve her goals. I was almost in tears as I spoke because just after I said that, I realized *I really was doing this race for my wife.* This may not be discipleship the way most people think of discipleship, but the dots were being connected in my life. Hoskins had been about coming alongside Johnny to help him achieve his God-given assignment. This was about coming alongside my wife.

COUER D'ALENE

That same night, one of my relatives, Michael Hoch, a multiple Ironman finisher, sent me an e-mail out of the blue that said, "Remember the race does not start until mile 80 on the bike." Kate and I read that e-mail without understanding what he meant. What was so special about mile 80 on the bike, we wondered? But we kept it in mind. Race day came quickly, and we went through our readiness routine, eating what we needed to eat, hitting Don's John for the last time, donning our wet suits, and *voilà*...we were on the beach, ready for the start. But this morning was different than most races. I was rushed. I did not have the time I typically had to see where we would be swimming, and for the first time in any race, I was wearing earplugs. Earplugs help keep your equilibrium intact in cold water, and since the water temperature in Couer d'Alene that day was 58 degrees, they were necessary. I could not hear anything between the loud music and the earplugs. I was flustered.

BOOM!

Kate and I prayed together, and then the cannon boomed. All of the 2,200-plus participants of the 2010 CDA Ironman plunged into the cold water at the same time to swim the 2.4 miles. Instantly, I was in a crowd of swimmers, but managed fairly well, considering all the feet kicking me. I swam for about a quarter mile before a thought came to my mind, out of the blue: had my chip been activated? The chip is what athletes wear during a race so the officials can track their progress. Typically, you walk over a mat and hear the beep from your chip indicating it is activated. No chip, no time; in other words, you are disqualified if you are not wearing an activated chip. I didn't remember walking over a mat because Kate and I took a shortcut to the beach in our rush. So I swam over to a volunteer who was on a kayak and asked him whether or not it was okay that my chip had not been activated. I didn't get the reassurance I had hoped for. The volunteer told me I needed to go back to activate my chip! Stunned and reluctant, but unwilling to risk an entire day racing to find out they had no record of me, I turned around and swam back to shore on the inside of the approaching swimmers. I had gone about a fourth of a mile before turning around. I don't know if you can imagine what it was like, but there I was, the only person swimming the wrong way in an Ironman!

SECOND START

About fifteen minutes after the start of the race, I was back on the shore earnestly searching for someone from the Ironman crew to tell me how to activate my chip. I must have looked like a frantic seal as I yelled for help in a full black wetsuit—anyway, the looks from the crowd indicated that is how I looked! Then I saw the wall I climbed over to get to the start of the race: it was lined with activation mats. My chip was activated. I was fine.

All my worries disappeared as quickly as they had come. Now I was just mad! I wondered what I had been thinking and what that volunteer had been thinking as well! I ran back into the water myself, sixteen minutes after the race had begun, to swim the same distance I had already done. As a Christian who had constantly prayed for this race, I was now asking God these questions:

"What is up with that little escapade? Aren't You supposed to be helping me here? I have been praying and praying and praying for a great race, a strong race, and a fast one for months, and here I am swimming longer than anyone else and starting sixteen minutes behind everyone else! Help me please! Where are You, God?"

Describing me as frustrated would have been an understatement! I was cold, mentally tired, alone, and sixteen minutes behind when I heard that small little voice inside my head say:

"Where is Kate? You will know why that 'escapade' happened later in the day. Don't worry about it; just swim!"

I immediately found peace and settled back into swimming. I didn't know what was coming, but I did know that had this not have happened, I may never have seen Kate in the race. Based upon our training, we went about the same pace in all events except swimming: I was the faster swimmer. This put me behind her. I transitioned to the bike without incident and began the 112-mile ride.

MILE 80

I caught Kate just after mile 80 on the bike, just when we had entered the Coeur d'Alene Mountains for the second time: there were two loops of fifty-six miles each. She was all cramped up (inside and out) and about to walk her bike. At the very time she wanted to get off her bike, and at the very time Michael had told us the race really started, mile 80, I showed up. I am sure he had no idea of the prophetic words of his e-mail, but now we did. I stayed by her side up and down the mountains, all the way to the finish of the bike. Then we ran the marathon together—all of it. As I was running, I was thinking about what I had said at the Rotary Club meeting—this was my wife's dream, and I was simply there to help her accomplish it.

It was not for me. But it required a total revamping of my life to come alongside Kate in this venture. Isn't this what discipleship is all about?

> Though I am free and belong to no one, I have made myself a slave to everyone, to win as many as possible. To the Jews I became like a Jew, to win the Jews. To those under the law I became like one under the law (though I myself am not under the law), so as to win those under the law. To those not having the law I became like one not having the law (though I am not free from God's law but am under Christ's law), so as to win those not having the law. To the weak I became weak, to win the weak. I have become all things to all people so that by all possible means I might save some. I do all this for the sake of the gospel, that I may share in its blessings (1 Corinthians 9:19-23).

To devote ourselves to those we disciple takes far more time and effort than many are willing to give. But what if this *is the model?* Or at least, what if this model is closer to true discipleship than the model we find in our Christian institutions today? If so, this issue alone will require a revamping of our lives.

CHAPTER 18
QUESTIONS

1. Do you love anyone enough to "change your entire routine" for their sake? Have you?

2. Who do you make time for?

3. Who won't you make time for?

4. What does it look like to make time for the people in your life who you say you love?

5. How many people is that?

19 Steps to Identify Your Calling

"If you don't know where you're going, any road
will take you there."
—George Harrison[63]

The sixth solution is knowing our individual calling. I don't mean the one that generically calls us to love others or help the poor. I mean the one that tells us our specific position in God's army so we know what we are supposed to do and not do with our life. The one that helps us accept an invitation or reject one that comes our way.

See to it that you complete the ministry you have received in the Lord (Colossians 4:17).

KNOWING YOUR POSITION

Laurie Beth Jones writes in her book, *The Path*, that during WWII if a soldier was confronted by other soldiers and did not know his orders, he risked being shot on the spot.[64] While most of us do not face a life-or-death situation regarding our God-given orders, it is still important that we know our role, position, and responsibilities (orders).

DISCOVERING YOUR PURPOSE

How do we find God's purpose and calling for our lives? There is no absolute standard to understanding a calling. A study of biblical characters makes it clear that there is no formula used for this. Some were certain of their calling, such as Noah, Abraham, Moses, the judges, the kings, the prophets, Zechariah, Elizabeth, Mary, John, Jesus, the disciples, and Paul. Some were called without knowing their call until it was fulfilled. Joseph is our best example, but there are others as well, such as Jacob and Esther. As these individuals were obedient to what they did know and to the leading of God, He established His plan in their lives. They did not have intimate foreknowledge about

---

63. Harrison, George, *Any Road*, performed by George Harrison (2002: London: Umlaut Corporation.) CD.

64. Jones, Laurie Beth. *The Path: Creating Your Mission Statement for Work and for Life*. New York: Hyperion, 1996. 9.

the plans God had for them. God may have been speaking in the silence of their hearts, but they did not have the blueprint, as some others did. Let me repeat that there is no consistent, absolute biblical process to understanding a calling, but the following steps might help you actually discover or affirm yours—at least they helped me discover mine since I did not have a "burning-bush" experience.

STEPS
The steps are:

1. Discover your spiritual gifts.

2. Remember your experiences.

3. Understand your passion.

4. Be honest about your strengths and weaknesses.

5. Write down your likes and dislikes.

6. Consider what you are doing and why you are doing it.

7. Decide what you would do if you had $5,000,000, no debt, and no fear.

8. Find Scripture references that support the calling you feel led to pursue and get affirmation.

9. Understand what important need you are fulfilling.

10. Trial and error.

11. Show up.

12. Pursue other biblical studies to deepen your relationship with Christ and for further affirmation or clarification.

SPIRITUAL GIFTS

First, I had to understand what my spiritual gifts were. Paul makes it clear that we all have different gifts and should use them in their fullness to serve the body of Christ.[65] There are various tests you can take to help you discover your spiritual gifts. A link is provided in the footnote on page 171 for a test

---

65. "Just as each of us has one body with many members, and these members do not all have the same function, so in Christ we who are many form one body, and each member belongs to all the others. We have different gifts, according to the grace given us. If a man's gift is prophesying, let him use it in proportion to his faith. If it is serving, let him serve; if it is teaching, let him teach; if it is encouraging, let him encourage; if it is contributing to the needs of others, let him give generously; if it is leadership, let him govern diligently; if is showing mercy, let him do it cheerfully" (Romans 12:3-8).

online. It is completely free, and you do not have to give personal information to take the test if you do not want to. You can register as a guest and just take the test. It will identify your top three gifts and show you a chart on how you scored on all of the gifts. It also has descriptive outlines of all the gifts, including administration, teaching, helps, etc. This is a very helpful tool.[66] The results will probably be consistent with what you already have seen as your strengths. If they are not, prayerfully consider possible reasons for this variance or find another gift test to take to see if the results are similar.

WHERE IS MY PASSION?

Second, I looked at my past experiences (my jobs, education, and hobbies) as an indicator of my calling. Did my experiences line up with my spiritual gifts? What had I done in my lifetime that might indicate what I was supposed to do now? (Take the time to write these past experiences down. After completing the spiritual gifts test, see if any of those gifts match with your experience.) *Third*, I had to consider my passion as part of my purpose. What got me up in the morning? What would I do whether I got paid for it or not?

STRENGTHS & WEAKNESSES

Fourth, I had to assess myself. Accurately knowing my strengths and weaknesses, particularly my weaknesses, was a great challenge to me, as it is to many people. But a healthy person must know both. Did you assess the stage disciple you are? That is part of this step. But it is more than that. Where do you struggle? Do you procrastinate or do you easily engage? Are you naturally empathetic to the needs of others or more self-absorbed? Are you a good listener or a better talker? Do you know how to delegate responsibility or do you prefer to do it yourself? Are you a builder or sustainer? Are you an organizer or do you need help with organization? Are you a visionary or do you support the vision of others? Assessing strengths and weaknesses is essential to fulfilling a God-given calling.

LIKES & DISLIKES

Fifth, I considered my likes and dislikes. These are often clues pointing to the ministry for which we are made. Sometimes, people are reluctant to discover their godly purpose because they are afraid it might involve something they don't like—such as having to go to Africa and live in a hut or move to the inner city. *Au contraire!* It's much more likely to be a plan of great delight.

---

66. "SpiritualGiftsTest.com." Adult Spiritual Gifts Test. Accessed October 4, 2015. Go to http://www.spiritualgiftstest.com/test/adult

God makes us with particular bents that are perfectly fitted for His plans, like a hand in a glove. We need not fear.

I made a list of the things I liked and disliked, including anything and everything, even my own contradictions—such as loving McDonald's food but also loving being in great physical shape. I also wanted to be debt free but kept spending money. I was forced to see my own contradictions as well as understand the things that really satisfy me deep down. Try this yourself, and be honest as you do.

CURRENT SITUATION

Sixth, I also looked at what I was currently doing—my present circumstances. I was where I was through some guidance, so I did not write off my current situation as irrelevant or out of line with my calling. I simply considered how I got there. If you are unemployed, what were you doing before now? And remember Romans 8:28 as you do: God uses all things for His glory and your good! Take a moment and think about what you would do if you could do anything you wanted. In other words, describe your perfect job. What would that be? This too, can be an indicator of your calling in life.

IF I HAD $5,000,000

Seventh, I considered what I would do if I had $5,000,000 and fear was not an issue. I decided it was to help the poor. When we eliminate money and fear as issues in our lives, it helps us understand what forces drive us. This may also help us to understand our calling more accurately. What would you do today if you had millions in the bank and didn't fear anything? (This is similar to your dream job.)

DOES IT AGREE WITH THE BIBLE AND IS IT AFFIRMED?

Eighth, I looked to see if what I felt called to do was supported by Scripture. It was. The Bible is focused on outreach rather than selfish gain. Any scriptural calling is supported by the Word of God. What Scripture supports the direction you feel led to follow? Henry & Richard Blackaby and Claude V. King remind us in *Experiencing God* that we should look to see where God is at work around us in an effort to "join Him." This is a way of doing just that: check the Scriptures, see where they intersect with your heart as part of your efforts to discover your calling.[67]

---

67. Blackaby, Henry T., and Claude V. King. *Experiencing God: How to Live the Full Adventure of Knowing and Doing the Will of God*. Nashville, Tenn.: Broadman & Holman Publishers, 1994. Unit 2.

Make sure it is also confirmed by wise counsel, bathed in prayer and that you fast throughout the process. Prayer, wise counsel, and fasting are essential elements to understanding our calling.

FASTING

Since fasting is an important part of this process, but is often overlooked, I want to discuss it just a bit here. In the book of Esther, an edict was made by the king to eliminate the Jewish population. In response, Queen Esther, who the king did not know was Jewish, made this plea to Mordecai, her guardian (Esther 2:7):

> Go and gather together all the Jews of Susa and fast for me. Do not eat or drink for three days, night or day. My maids and I will do the same. And then, though it is against the law, I will go in to see the king. If I must die, I must die (Esther 4:16).

Queen Esther's life was spared and she saved the Jewish people. She had been prepared by God for "such a time as this."[68] Evidently fasting mattered in that instance. In Daniel, it says that Daniel had to fast for three weeks in order for God's angelic help to reach him:

> When this vision came to me, I, Daniel, had been in mourning for three whole weeks. All that time I had eaten no rich food. No meat or wine crossed my lips, and I used no fragrant lotions until those three weeks had passed (Daniel 10:2-3).

> Then he said, "Don't be afraid, Daniel. Since the first day you began to pray for understanding and to humble yourself before your God, your request has been heard in heaven. I have come in answer to your prayer. But for twenty-one days the spirit prince of the kingdom of Persia blocked my way. Then Michael, one of the archangels, came to help me, and I left him there with the spirit prince of the kingdom of Persia. Now I am here to explain what will happen to your people in the future, for this vision concerns a time yet to come" (Daniel 10:12-14 NLT).

Jesus fasted for forty days in the wilderness and said "when you fast" rather than "if you fast" to all of us (Matthew 6:16). My many experiences with fasting suggest it is something Christians should regularly do to draw closer

---

68. Esther 4:14.

to God and hear Him more clearly. Knowing our orders should be important enough for us to take advantage of this spiritual discipline.

WISE COUNSEL

Many people are used to making decisions in a vacuum or with people who either don't know them personally or are unable to give wise counsel. Have other mature Christians affirmed you in the area you are feeling led to pursue? Having affirmation will hold you steady later on when you may be under attack. This ties in with the need to have a person discipling you. When we have such a person in our life, they should know us well enough to affirm or challenge our direction. Having confirmation you are following the plan of God for your life will grant you great confidence.

FILLING A NEED

Ninth, I have heard some say our purpose can be found where we see the world's greatest need intersecting with our desire to fill it. Many of us can identify specific needs in the world that we care about. Mine was helping the homeless. Is there a problem in the world that you want to help resolve? That should be a direction finder to your calling. One caution: we should not get involved in something we might hear about or see on television just because it pokes at our feelings. *This is one indicator, but may not be **the** indicator.* Take it in stride with these other issues.

TRIAL AND ERROR

Tenth is trial and error. Sometimes we can be so afraid of failing that we won't take risks. Years ago, I heard a sermon that seemed to confirm this point. The speaker, John Tolson, said that a group of ninety-five-year-old men were asked what they would do differently if they could live their lives over again.[69] The second point on their list of three points was risk: they would have taken more risks. Faith is connected to risk. Abraham was called to leave his country, his family, and go to a place God would reveal. Scripture says he set out for Canaan. It also says he arrived there. He took a chance and trusted God to show him where to go. Moses also took a risk: he returned to Egypt, the same nation he had fled forty years before. Later, the Israelites were afraid of the giants in the Promised Land and none of them made it there except for the two who had faith: Joshua and Caleb. I volunteered in several areas of ministry while God fine-tuned my own calling. Walk by faith. Take risks.

---

69. Their first point was to reflect more; second, to take more risks; and last, to invest in things that would outlive them.

SHOW UP

Eleventh, I needed to show up. This is why I checked myself into the Uptown Men's Shelter. Perhaps you need to go on a mission trip, or work at a shelter, or join the church helping needy families. Whatever the situation, just show up. You cannot do anything until you get your hands dirty. *Where do you feel led to show up?*

EXPERIENCING GOD

Finally, I did biblically based study guides. My first and favorite was the aforementioned *Experiencing God* by Henry Blackaby and Claude V. King. After completing *Experiencing God*[70] I continued with the Master-life series, which includes the following titles:

The Disciple's Cross[71]

The Disciple's Personality[72]

The Disciple's Victory[73]

The Disciple's Mission[74]

There are other good studies as well. Find the ones that best fit your personality, that you feel the Holy Spirit is leading you to pursue, and complete them. If you are married, consider doing them with your spouse.

Finally, I read *The Path* by Laurie Beth Jones[75] and completed the exercises in the book. Whatever materials you choose, I highly suggest you seek your calling by looking into this further.

CAUTIONS

I would be remiss if I didn't caution about the potential to miss our calling if we do not exercise faith once we do understand what it is, or if we are disobedient. Remember, we always have a choice. Isaiah heard the voice of the Lord say, "Whom shall I send? And who will go for us?" To which Isaiah responded, "Here I am. Send me!" It is clear from Jesus' own words that many are called but few are chosen.[76] Perhaps many of us are being asked that same question today: will we go or not? Will we follow that slight tug on our hearts

70. Blackaby, Henry T., and Claude V. King. *Experiencing God: How to Live the Full Adventure of Knowing and Doing the Will of God*. Nashville, Tenn.: Broadman & Holman Publishers, 1994.

71. Willis, Avery T., and Kay Moore. *The Disciple's Cross*. Nashville, Tn.: LifeWay Press, 1996.

72. Willis, Avery T., and Kay Moore. *The Disciple's Personality*. Nashville, Tn.: LifeWay Press, 1996.

73. Willis, Avery T., and Kay Moore. *The Disciple's Victory*. Nashville, Tn.: LifeWay Press, 1996.

74. Willis, Avery T., and Kay Moore. *The Disciple's Mission*. Nashville, Tn.: LifeWay Press, 1997.

75. Jones, Laurie Beth. The Path: Creating Your Mission Statement for Work and for Life. New York: Hyperion, 1996.

that suggests God is calling us to go and do something? Love demands a choice, by definition. That means we all have a choice to make regarding our calling. Do you know what God has asked you to do? Then do it.

NO DETAILED CALLING?

Finally, if we do not believe we have a detailed calling such as building an ark, we must simply live the way we are "called" to live in God's Word. Joseph is our best Old Testament illustration of this point. He did what he was taught to do and had faith that God would take care of him. Micah tells us what the Lord requires of us:

> He has showed you, O man, what is good. And what does the Lord require of you? To act justly and to love mercy and to walk humbly with your (Micah 6:8).

We also know we are called to make disciples:

> Therefore go and make disciples of all nations, baptizing them in the name of the Father and of the Son and of the Holy Spirit (Matthew 28:19).

That means we need to know just who our disciples really are. Do you know? That is our next topic. But try not to rush to the next chapter without answering the upcoming questions! This is important and could change your life.

---

76. Matthew 22:1ff, Luke 13:34, Luke 14:16-23.

CHAPTER 19
QUESTIONS

1. What are your spiritual gifts?

2. List your past experiences, education, and hobbies.

3. What are you passionate about?

4. What are you good at?

5. Where do you need help?

6. What do you like? What do you dislike?

7. What are you currently doing?

8. Describe the perfect job for you.

9. If you had $5,000,000, what would you do differently?

10. What Scripture supports what you want to do?

11. Have you prayed about your calling? Have you fasted?

12. What is your calling?

13. Have you been affirmed by those qualified to affirm you? Why or why not?

20 How to Discover Your Disciples

"Simple doesn't mean stupid. Thinking that it does, does."
—Paul Krugman

The seventh and final solution is discovering who we are called to disciple. It doesn't have to be twelve, but saying we have more than twelve puts us at odds with one of the previously mentioned solutions—as well as putting us at odds with Jesus! These disciples are the few people we should be pouring our life into on a daily or weekly basis. They are very important to the fulfillment of our calling. Keep in mind that a disciple is someone who has committed his or her life to Jesus. We cannot officially disciple a non-believer—but we can and must love non-believers as part of the evangelism process by modeling Jesus in all our dealings with them. One will have to discern who God wants us to spend time with regarding the process of conversion as it intersects with the process of discipleship. It can be a very fine line. One thing for sure, we won't have the time to "do it all." If we are evangelizing many non-believers, we need to ensure the process of discipleship is intact once they become Christians. One will also need to know just how much effort to put into those who refuse Jesus as Lord and Savior throughout the process. As we will see in the upcoming obstacle section, the entire model falls apart when a person is trying to do too much, with too many. There is no simple way to know besides letting God tell you, Himself. That means staying connected to the vine of Christ. As Christians we must be able to hear from God:

> My sheep hear my voice, and I know them, and they follow me (John 10:27 ESV)

THE IMPORTANCE OF FAMILY

Pastor Rob Rienow was the typical spiritual leader at his church. As a pastor he was busy discipling other people at the expense of his own family. After a time of understanding and repentance, he and his wife Amy launched

179

Visionary Family Ministries in an effort to equip the church to grow through a global reformation of family discipleship.[77] Now he says this about a pastor's true role:

> "A pastor must first think of himself as a Christian individual, called by God to walk in prayer, Scripture, personal holiness, compassion, and filled with evangelistic fervor. Second, a pastor must then live out his faith in the context of his family. Does he have parents? His faith begins with his honor and care for them. Does he have siblings? Does he love them, serve them, and seek to partner with them for the gospel? Is he married? God calls him to love, serve, and lead his wife as his most important ministry. Is he a father or grandfather? God has seen fit to entrust immortal souls into his care, and those souls require his most fervent prayers, evangelism, discipleship, training, and equipping. He opens his home as a place of ministry to his neighbors and to his fellow Christians. He does not do these things because he is a pastor, but because he is a Christian!"[78]

Our good works cannot consume us while we preach against them—at the expense of those closest to us. One pastor I know had a growing church and woke up to a new reality when his wife left him. It is difficult for any of us to stay well-balanced in life, let alone a pastor. But we must—especially pastors. If the family model is so important in life, then *sacrificing our family for the sake of some greater good is simply a tactic of our enemy.*

OUR FIRST DISCIPLES ARE FOUND IN OUR FAMILY

The first of our disciples are our family members. I have always been curious why many church leaders seem to want all of the single people in their churches to be married. Jesus wasn't married—nor was Paul—and neither promote marriage in the Bible. In fact, Paul says to avoid it if you can! Jesus says be prepared—it won't be easy! Anyone reading this who is married understands. It is beautiful, but comes with its challenges. It is also clear that this institution can distract us from a focus on ministry:

> But I desire to have you to be free from cares. He who is unmarried is concerned for the things of the Lord, how he may please the Lord;

77. "Visionary Family Ministries." Visionary Family Ministries Rob and Amy Rienow Comments. Accessed October 4, 2015.
78. Rienow, Rob. *Limited Church: Unlimited Kingdom: Uniting Church and Family in the Great Commission.* Nashville, TN: Randall House, 2013. 121.

but he who is married is concerned about the things of the world, how he may please his wife. There is also a difference between a wife and a virgin. The unmarried woman cares about the things of the Lord, that she may be holy both in body and in spirit. But she who is married cares about the things of the world—how she may please her husband. This I say for your own profit; not that I may ensnare you, but for that which is appropriate, and that you may attend to the Lord without distraction (1 Corinthians 7:31-35).

We cannot have it all, like our culture appears to believe. It doesn't work in the world and it doesn't work in the church. Our first disciples are our immediate family members. If we are married, this starts with our spouses. It is not enough to consider our spouse as our partner and friend. Our spouse must be our number one disciple; each one of us is a soul being transformed by God. The more difficult the spouse, the less time we have to disciple others. That is why our choice of a spouse is so important to our calling and ministry. It is also why we should do everything possible to avoid divorce. Divorce might just be a version of firing Judas.

OUR SECOND SET OF DISCIPLES IS FOUND AT WORK

Once we have assessed our family, we can see who God has put in our lives to disciple at work, where many of us spend a good deal of our time. One glance at the pie chart you created earlier can verify if this is true or not for you. We probably spend a good amount of time with a small group of people at work, even if we don't like them and even if we don't define them as a "small group." Have you considered whether God wants you to be in a discipleship relationship with any of them? If we are on a leadership team of some sort, those are the people that we influence most and who influence us in turn. Do you have a business partner? Perhaps that person is on your list. How about other leaders you work with at your job? Or other board members if you are serving on a board of directors? They might be on your list. If you are not in an official leadership position, look at your peers. Are any of them thirsty for Jesus? Are any of them visibly searching for God? Who are they? They cannot be searching for God without God being at work in them.

No one can come to me unless the Father who sent me draws them (John 6:44).

CLOSE FRIENDS AND NEIGHBORS

Most of us know that close friends are few and far between. Social media might appear to increase the number of friends in our lives, but it really just increases our acquaintances and could actually hurt our closest relationships. Many people come and go in our lives, but friends stick with us. In fact, that may be how we know who our friends really are: who has stuck with us? They are often on our list of twelve. That would include those in your church small group.

The next group is our neighbors. This might be one of our most neglected groups: the people who live next door to us. You know, the ones we scurry away from on a daily basis as we make our way to work and church. It is only natural that we would grow and blossom in the soil of the place in which God has directed us to put down our roots. Our neighbors are part of the field God has placed us in, and are potential people to disciple. Put the ones who stand out on your list.

THE POOR

The Bible defines the poor as orphans, widows, the homeless, and those living in poverty. If you added up twelve people through the previous examples, you are now faced with the issue I have with modern-day Christianity and our desire to help the poor:

- Can we effectively *disciple* those we meet who are "poor"?

- Do we have the time?

- If we cannot, how do we decide what help to give them?

The story of the Good Samaritan implies we need to help those who are in immediate need. What the Good Samaritan did was an example of relief as defined by Steve Corbett and Brian Fikkert in *When Helping Hurts*, and not rehabilitation or development. The same is true with this passage from James:

> Suppose you see a brother or sister who has no food or clothing, and you say, "Good-bye and have a good day; stay warm and eat well"— but then you don't give that person any food or clothing. What good does that do? (James 2:15-16 NLT)

If we attempt to do more with this person without the time, training, or calling, could we not be undermining the entire issue of discipleship with those for whom we do have the time to disciple—those, in fact, God has assigned to us? When we are spread too thin to help them to the degree necessary, we become part of the problem we are trying to fix. Our focus is diminished. We can still help—but not at the discipleship level. Most of us fill up our twelve through our families, our workplace, our small groups, and our neighbors. We have no ability to help the poor to the degree we may desire because we do not understand the need and we do not have the time. A review of "Chapter 9: Unrealistic Expectations and a Wrong Definition of Success," and "Chapter 18: Discipleship Requires Time—Do We Have Enough?" will remind us of that.

We must understand who is called to disciple the poor and help them to do it more effectively. Adopt a leader helping the poor, make sure they are in their proper role with built-in accountability to biblically based boundaries as we have discussed, and support them at a high level.

Christians cannot deal with people like a business and say we are following biblical teachings or the Holy Spirit. Instead, we should understand our calling and recognize that the people we are called to invest our lives in need us—all of us. Discipleship is not part-time work. When God puts others in our life who have an affirmed calling and who are appropriately trained to help others who "don't look like us," we should come alongside them before we try to be them without the same calling, experience, or training. At the very minimum we should include them in a discipleship process if we still feel God is calling us to dive into the life of someone whose culture is different from our own.

Those are the solutions to the AHA moments I struggled with once I moved into urban America. Before we conclude I want to discuss potential obstacles we will face implementing these solutions. Everything is easier said than done and this is no exception. Consider the following issues as ways the enemy will use to trip us up, even the most mature Christians among us:

• A focus on numbers

• A lack of time

• Our lifestyle

• Not recognizing that we are in a war

• A faulty definition of success

It is to these topics we now turn.

CHAPTER 20
QUESTIONS

If you are married, write your spouse's name:

_____

If you have children (or other relatives), list them:_____

_____

_____

_____

_____

_____

If you have grandchildren, list them: _____

_____

_____

_____

_____

_____

If you are a leader in an organization, list either your partner or leadership team here. If you are an employee in an organization or company, list those to whom you are closest in your office:

_____

_____

_____

_____

_____

List your close friends: _____

_____

_____

_____

_____

_____

List your neighbors: _____

_____

_____

_____

_____

_____

If you exercise (or have a hobby), list those with whom you consistently meet:_____

_____

_____

_____

_____

_____

List others in your life with whom you spend a fair amount of time: _____

_____

_____

_____

_____

Based upon your answers, who do you think are your disciples?

_____

_____

_____

_____

If you have more than twelve, what steps will you take to modify your list? _____

_____

_____

_____

_____

_____

_____

_____

_____

PART FOUR

OBSTACLES

WHAT WILL PREVENT US FROM FULFILLING THE CALL GOD HAS ON OUR LIFE?

21

Focusing on Width Rather Than Depth

"We cannot go a mile wide and an inch deep in community development, because these are people, not projects."
—Jen Hatmaker[79]

The first obstacle to implementing the solutions we discussed is a prideful focus on numbers. If discipleship is truly Christian training for the sake of life transformation, and we are watching America fall from grace, then we need to know how many people we can effectively disciple. Even though we already spent time revealing "our twelve," most likely we have not fine-tuned that number. We need to do that. Here's why.

TOYOTA

Since its inception, Toyota understood the importance of producing great cars. Because of the company's dedication to superior quality and innovation, it surpassed General Motors as the world's largest car maker in 2008. Toyota built great cars and everyone knew it. Several years ago, however, the company's quality control was challenged by its desire to produce cheaper cars.[80] Quality control takes more time, and therefore costs more money. In Toyota's desire to reduce costs and increase profits, it produced more than 14 million defective cars.[81] Some had acceleration and brake defects and were involved in fatal accidents. Toyota produced more cars, but some drivers died in the name of "productivity." Could the churches that focus on numbers be producing defective Christians? Or are they becoming the church version of Octomom?

NADYA SULEMAN

Many remember Nadya Suleman as Octomom. She was single, in her thirties, and had fourteen kids. After having six kids, she spent an estimated $24,000[82] on the in-vitro procedure to have eight more: thus the title Octomom. She

79. Hatmaker, Jen. *For the Love: Fighting for Grace in a World of Impossible Standards.* Nashville, TN: Nelson Books, 2015.
80. "Toyota Production System." Wikipedia. Accessed November 27, 2015. https://en.wikipedia.org/wiki/Toyota_Production_System.
81. http://topics.nytimes.com/top/news/business/companies/toyota_motor_corporation/index.html
82. In her latest interview with Life & Style Magazine, Nadya Sulemann says she paid $24,000 for in vitro fertilization for her first four children, with her $30,000 inheritance, along with money from OT working in her job as Psych Tech.

became financially strained, and lived on food stamps, getting about $490 per month from the government, with three disabled children, which allowed her to collect disability as well.[83] Although most of us would consider what she did to be abnormal, she still did it. The issue now is what will be the result of her choices for the kids and who is going to pay for her decisions? Since she is single, that automatically puts the kids at a disadvantage, statistically speaking, because they typically end up in poverty.

Most parents understand why it is better for a child to have two people looking after that child rather than just one. And this woman has fourteen! That is enough to overwhelm a healthy, normal (whatever normal really is) couple, and unthinkable for a single parent. The bottom line: having fourteen kids put all of them at immediate risk. That's what I think we might be doing when we choose to disciple more people than is possible. We need to be very careful that we are not growing a flock at the expense of our calling:

> Even some men from your own group will rise up and distort the truth in order to draw a following. Watch out! (Acts 20:30)

UNDERCOVER BOSS

If you have ever watched the television show, *Undercover Boss*, you know that whenever the president or CEO of an organization goes undercover and works with employees down the food chain, that same leader is shocked by what he or she discovers. Founder and CEO Rick Forman of Forman Mills, one of the fastest-growing discount clothing stores in the country, went undercover as Brad Bandini in his own organization. Sales associate Mshinda shared with Brad that the price check system in Forman Mills was outdated. As a result, Rick replaced the entire system in his company and promoted Mshinda to merchandise co-ordinator, giving her a $25,000 raise. He also sent her family on a vacation to Disney World and paid the cost for the next five years of education for her kids when he found out how challenged she was financially and by time constraints. Then Brad found out that Nikia lived in the projects with a special-needs child. He gave her an immediate $17,000 raise plus $15,000 per child to get her out of government housing. Kurtis aspired to be a warehouse manager and was doing everything he could to earn that promotion. During lunch, he invited Brad to go with him to the local shelter, something Kurtis did regularly. As a result of his time with Kurtis, Mr. Forman promoted Kurtis to warehouse manager,

---

83. "Nadya Suleman." Wikipedia. Accessed November 27, 2015. https://en.wikipedia.org/wiki/Nadya_Suleman.

doubled his salary, gave him $250,000 for a house, and started an outreach to the poor for Forman Mills that he asked Kurtis to lead. Based upon his entire undercover experience, Mr. Forman decided to start profit-sharing for all employees and set aside $1,000,000 each year for further community outreach. These are some of the comments he has made about going undercover:

- "It's about the people. Today is the first day of the rest of our business."

- "I found really good people who come to work every day. The job means everything to them. It's not just a business, it's a community."

- "They are great people, and I don't think they know they have a gift. *I don't think we're nurturing them.*"

- "*I need to spend more time with the people in the trenches.*"[84]

All Rick had to do was get to know his employees by spending more time with them. Although it cost him financially, he made profound discoveries about his employees and himself: They needed more time and nurturing—the heart of the issues of Christian discipleship. We all need time and nurturing from those who are important or significant in our lives. But what leader at what size organization has the time to do this? If we have become a Christian version of Octomom or Octodad, we don't.

The larger the organization, the higher the boss is over its lower-tier employees and the more likely the boss is to lose touch with those employees. Once it becomes a bureaucracy, more and more boundaries are put into place, and the organization becomes more political with less concern for one employee. The process becomes more mechanical. This is happening in our churches.

FRANCIS CHAN

Francis Chan, preacher and author of the bestselling book, *Crazy Love*, understands the impact numbers are having on our Christian institutions and is doing church differently. Besides his own inner spirit compelling him to give more of his finances and disciple fewer people at a deeper level, Chan went to China where he experienced the home church movement.[85] He noticed how passionate the people were for Christ overseas, while the church in America has become more complacent. A prominent pastor himself, with a congregation of more than 4,000 (Cornerstone Church in Simi Valley, California), he felt compelled to bring the home church model of China to the US:

---

84. "Forman Mills." In *Undercover Boss*. CBS. May 22, 2015.

85. Chan, Francis, and Danae Yankoski. *Crazy Love: Overwhelmed by a Relentless God.* Colorado Springs, Colo.: David C. Cook, 2008.

"The Lord said to me, 'You didn't finish what you were supposed to do in the United States. I want you to change the way we do church.'" [86]

He left his big church in California and is now modeling the *early church home church model*, meeting in the homes of his congregants with this message:

"I am not going to preach on Sundays. We are all going to read the Bible together during the week. Church has to be less about going to the movies and more like going to the gym." [87]

Every six to twelve months, as his home churches grow, they split and continue to follow the same model: more investment in fewer people. That is how he has felt led to do church differently:

"I don't know how on earth anyone's going to survive leading a church in the future and staying Biblical. With the amount of criticism and flattery we get through social media, it is a big challenge to remain humble rather than angry, arrogant, or depressed. And I don't see how churches can maintain the current financial structure. It is time to pioneer something new. That is what we are doing." [88]

While sitting at Starbucks, a mother and son sat down at my table. I could not help but overhear what the mother was telling her son: "I am 74 years old," she said, obviously frustrated. "I'd rather be hit by a bus than stay there for the next twenty years. You have no idea." Evidently one of her children was trying to put her in a retirement home, and she didn't want to live there. The son at my table said very little; he appeared to just listen to his mother. Most of the important people in our lives need more time than most of us have to give them. We don't have to be pastors to recognize that we need to be careful how many people we can effectively love. Trying to care for too many people can prevent us from fulfilling God's call on our lives.

Focus. Discern your disciples. Then invest your time in them.

---

86. "Doing Church a Different Way—Francis Chan, Bestselling Author." Finding God in Silicon Valley. November 12, 2013. Accessed October 1, 2015.
87. Ibid.
88. Ibid.

CHAPTER 21 QUESTIONS

1. How do you react when you learn about the real need of another struggling person?

2. Can you see why a large number of people can hide the real needs of struggling people?

3. Who do you spend enough time with to truly understand their needs, whether they be emotional needs, spiritual needs, financial needs, or other?

4. What are the obvious problems in Christianity with a model that includes large numbers of people?

5. How many people do you think you are supposed to disciple? Would you consider yourself the average or do you think that number is true of just about everyone?

22 We Don't Have Time

"No man is greater than his prayer life."
—Leonard Ravenhill[89]

The second obstacle preventing us from the aforementioned solutions is a lack of time. It coattails on the last obstacle discussed: numbers. This will also be a reminder of the approach I felt God wanted me to take with Johnny. I had to come alongside of Johnny. That meant moving in next door to him and helping him at a pace suitable to his own walk with God—not mine. Below, I want to make a similar correlation about commitment using my Ironman events and coming alongside my wife. I want to use this to parallel the stages of discipleship we reviewed in chapter 14:

1. Commitment, repentance, and adjustments

2. Development, guidance, and involvement: "Learning about the One who gave me new life"

3. Growth in the body of Christ and personal discernment

4. Ministry development and testing

5. Further testing: "Learning to depend on Christ"

6. Ministry in the power of Christ

7. Maturity in Christ: "Fruit through the fullness of Christ"

IRONMAN TRAINING

As mentioned, an Ironman Triathlon is a 2.4-mile swim, followed by a 112-mile bike ride, followed by a full marathon. It encompasses 140.6 miles in a day. It is a long day. Since I believe all Christian leaders are in a spiritual Ironman, this illustration will help us gain a healthy perspective on our discipleship process. The longer and tougher the race, the more important it is to train appropriately and follow a guide: someone with experience.

89. To hear Leonard Ravenhill speak on this, go to https://www.youtube.com/watch?v=GVsVhZCJmtU.

As Christians living in very dark times, we need to understand that a la-di-da attitude will not get us to the end of this race. There may be nothing new under the sun (Ecclesiastes 1:9), but technology has brought the enemy into our homes via our smart phones, computers, and television sets. And our kids are at risk, as are we all.

STAGE ONE

Stage one for completing an Ironman is signing up for it. It begins with commitment. Most Ironman events fill up in a couple weeks, some in a couple minutes, so you have to know a year in advance whether you are willing to commit. Besides committing to a date, you have to pay to participate. Despite my strong belief that anyone who does an Ironman should be paid to do it, the opposite is true; it costs upwards of $500. It is not cheap. And there are other costs. It requires a decent bike; 112 miles is too much for an ordinary bike. This can be the difference between success and failure. And so, just as stage one in discipleship is a commitment to Christ and a change in behavior, stage one in an Ironman is a commitment to the race, which is likely to bring about many changes in behavior. The successive stages in an Ironman are all about the training and changes you go through in order to reach the final stage—stage seven, which is the Ironman race itself.

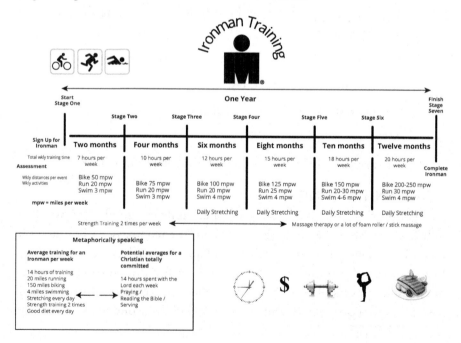

STAGES TWO TO SEVEN

As you see in the illustration, the amount of weekly training started out at roughly seven hours in stage one and progressed to twenty hours weekly for the last two months or stage seven. The amount of biking, running, and swimming increased accordingly through each stage. In stages four through seven, daily stretching, weekly massages, and strength training were imperative (although strength training should be reduced the last four weeks of stage seven to avoid injury). When and if I did not adhere to this schedule of stretching and strength training, I would get hurt. And believe me, I tried to avoid this stringent training at times—and did deal with injuries as a result. Strength training and stretching were not optional for me, especially since I was fifty years old. And while debates continue about good nutrition, it is not debatable to an Ironman. You either have it right or you don't. Ironman participants know their bodies. They know their food, and they know they have to put the right fuel in their bodies to train. If your nutrition is not in line with your training, your training will suffer.

SPIRITUAL CONNECTION

To make this relevant, let's look at the essentials of our life in Christ. Pastor Jim Kalam reminds Christians of our need to read and study God's Word, pray, and live in community:

> "God's Word *must* be taught. It's foundational. Prayer must be encouraged. It's essential. Community, however, cannot be forgotten: It *must* be pursued. It's indispensable. As we've moved through time, churches have typically emphasized one of these at the expense of the other. But *all three need to be pursued.*"[90]

While in community, we also need to serve one another and the less fortunate. This is found in the aforementioned passage from the book of Acts (2:42-47), as well as in this passage from the book of James:

> Real religion, the kind that passes muster before God the Father, is this: Reach out to the homeless and loveless in their plight, and guard against corruption from the godless world (James 1:27 MSG).

TIME FOR SPIRITUAL IRONMAN

Implied is that we worship God through our joyful participation in these areas: teaching/hearing the Word, praying, living and serving in community, and loving

---

90. Kalam, Jr., Jim. *Risking Church.* Charlotte, NC: Kalam Press, 2003. 81.

the poor. That means our Spiritual Ironman consists of the following activities, which I am averaging out to fourteen hours per week for purposes of our example. (This is not a rule, but meant to shed light on the reality of our walk.):

1. Prayer—30 minutes each day

2. Reading the Bible—30 minutes each day

3. Living and serving in community—30 minutes each day

4. Serving the poor—30 minutes each day

Translated, a potential measurement for whether or not a person is serious about their walk with Christ can be seen in how well they are practicing these disciplines. Spending two hours per day (or fourteen hours per week) praying, reading the Bible, living and serving in community (in non-business / family interaction) and serving the poor would be considered normal. These are the weapons we are supposed to use as we fight in this war:

> For though we live in the world, we do not wage war as the world does. The weapons we fight with are not the weapons of the world. On the contrary, they have divine power to demolish strongholds (2 Corinthians 10:3-4).

GUIDELINES

It goes without saying that we will sacrifice at least ten percent of our money to support this effort. This is a boundary to be prayed over and individually discerned, but taken seriously by those who are serious about fulfilling their God-given destiny. We cannot do as we please and still hit God's target. It's just like a marriage. Marriage is typically brought about by feelings, but marriage is *kept* together by commitment. Stop spending time with your spouse and your relationship fades. Depend on your feelings to guide the time you spend with your spouse and you will likely find yourself divorced. There are no rules that govern a good marriage, but there are guidelines to help keep us on track in a world that continues to lure us away from God. Christianity is the same way.

> I am saying this for your benefit, not to put restrictions on you (1 Corinthians 7:35 NLT).

Consider these points to help make my case:

- The American Heart Association recommends that the average person perform thirty minutes of moderately intensive aerobic exercise at least five times a week to maintain good health.

- For lowering blood pressure and cholesterol, the American Heart Association recommends forty minutes of moderate- to vigorous-intensity aerobic exercise three or four times per week.

- Researchers followed 34,000 middle-aged women for thirteen years and found that women who began the study in the normal weight range needed the equivalent of one hour a day of physical activity to stay at a steady weight.[91]

- The Food and Drug Administration requires food manufacturers to label their products because they know a healthy diet promotes good health.

None of these are hard and fast rules. The wise hear these healthy guidelines and take them to heart. If we follow them, we are typically blessed with good health. If we defy them, we may eventually be burdened with health problems. Rules have nothing to do with healthy suggestions. It is a known fact that the average American spends five hours each day watching television. If you are a parent, you will probably prevent your child from watching that much television because you know it will come at the expense of more important uses of their time. It is a form of discipline to monitor and stop such behavior. And discipline is required for a healthy, well-rounded life:

Discipline your children while there is hope. Otherwise you will ruin their lives (Proverbs 19:18).

I just listened to a short sermon called "Agony" by Leonard Ravenhill (1907-1994).[92] It is his belief that 95% of us are spiritually crippled, spiritual infants—children full of self-pity, self-interest, self-seeking, self-concern, me-first. He believed that five minutes inside eternity, every one of us will regret that we didn't sacrifice more, pray more, grieve more, weep more, and love more.[93]

What if he is right?

Consider these suggestions as self-imposed boundaries for a healthier spiritual life. If you are in a leadership position in a Christian organization and don't have the time to spiritually train as if you were in a Spiritual Ironman you and your flock will suffer.

Time is an obstacle to God's call on our lives.

91. Lee, I. M. et al. "Physical Activity and Weight Gain Prevention." National Center for Biotechnology Information. March 24, 2010. Accessed October 4, 2015. 173-9.

92. https://www.youtube.com/watch?v=Uv59vWZfJB0

93. https://www.youtube.com/watch?v=fes3sD_aLks

CHAPTER 22
QUESTIONS

1. What is your reaction to the information in this chapter?

2. Do you think Christians in today's culture are in a spiritual Ironman? Are you in one?

3. Reading the Word and spending time in prayer are both examples of conversation with the God who created us. Since that is true, why do you think we struggle to spend time with Him?

4. Do you think you spend enough time in prayer? If not, will you commit to praying more? If so, who will hold you accountable?

5. How much time do you spend at work? What would happen if you worked the same amount of time you spend with God? Would you have a job?

23 Our Lifestyle

> "For many of us the great danger is not that we will renounce our faith. It is that we will become so distracted and rushed and preoccupied that we will settle for a mediocre version of it."
> —John Ortberg[95]

The third obstacle is our lifestyle. Perhaps one of the most antagonistic things to say to an American is that he or she cannot have it all since most of us believe that the America Dream is about that: having it all. But this belief is one of the most destructive of our culture. Why? Because despite appearances, we can't have it all, and we might just spend our entire lives proving that point and missing the real reason we were put here in the first place. We are soldiers and must resist getting caught up in the affairs of the world in which we live:

> Endure suffering along with me, as a good soldier of Christ Jesus. Soldiers don't get tied up in the affairs of civilian life, for then they cannot please the officer who enlisted them (2 Timothy 2:3-4 NLT).

Many of us take jobs for the sake of an income that *we think we need to make us happy to maintain our lifestyle*. We *need* to live in a large house in a prominent neighborhood. We *need* to send our kid to an expensive school. We *need* to color coordinate the best kitchen appliances. We *need* a flat screen television set. We *need* to have a hundred television stations to choose from. We *need* a new car. We *need* to have the latest clothes. We *need* to go to Starbucks every day for our coffee fix. But read this from the book of Jeremiah:

> From the least to the greatest, their lives are ruled by greed. Yes, even my prophets and priests are like that. They are all frauds (Jeremiah 8:10 NLT).

Are we in a similar state today? Think about it.

---

95. Kroeker, Ann S. *Not so Fast: Slow-down Solutions for Frenzied Families*. Colorado Springs, CO: David C. Cook, 2009. 45.

PAST WANTS—TODAY'S NEEDS

We take jobs to have things despite our natural God-given gifts, despite the calling God has on our life, and despite what will truly make us happy. That is why most people *do die with their dreams still in them:* because they followed the wrong dream while on earth. Should we really put our kids in childcare so that both parents can work to sustain our lifestyles at the expense of those same kids? Should we stay at a job even if it is distancing us from our spouse? Is it right not to have time to spend with our next-door neighbors? Can we really blame our stress on something other than our chosen lifestyle? And doesn't that mean money is our master? Wasn't that true of Judas?[96]

THE FAMILY MAN

A good example of connecting the dots about this is found in the movie *The Family Man.*[97] Jack Campbell (played by Nicolas Cage) is a ruthless, rich, suave, single, Wall Street executive working on a billion-dollar business deal that will make everyone millions of dollars, including himself. Jack seems to have it all. As the story goes, he is mysteriously given a glimpse of the life he *didn't choose* several years earlier. As part of this mysterious dreamlike glimpse, Jack wakes up one morning married to his college sweetheart, Kate Reynolds (played by Teá Leoni) the girl he *almost married* years ago but chose not to because of a job opportunity overseas. She had wanted him to stay with her in the States, telling him just before he boarded his flight to London that she chose them over her own independence, and wanted him to do the same by staying. He decided to go to London anyway, telling her that their relationship would make it whether he moved or not. But he was wrong. Their relationship ended and that was that. But in this glimpse, to his surprise, he finds he is now married to Kate, has two adorable but young and *time-consuming* children, and works as a tire salesman at a tire company that his father-in-law owns called Big Ed's. In the dream, Jack passed up the job in London to marry Kate, as she had wanted him to do.

It is the antithesis of his real life.

COUNT THE COST

At first, Jack struggles with this change of life, mainly because he is no longer in control of things the way he appeared to be in his former life. But over time, he falls back in love with Kate and the kids, and he realizes just what

---

96. Henry, Matthew. "Mark 14 Commentary—Matthew Henry Commentary on the Whole Bible (Complete)." Bible Study Tools. Accessed October 15, 2015.

97. *The Family Man.* Directed by Brett Ratner. Universal Studios, 2000. Film.

he gave up by focusing on money, power, and personal comfort. He was giving up love—true and satisfying love—the thing that fuels our lives and makes them meaningful. What he thought would make him happy—fame, fortune, independence, big deals, expensive clothes, and romance—was unable to compete with the glimpse of life that he had with a family he loved. The dream finally ends, and Jack returns to his old life. Once again, he is the rich, single, Wall Street executive working the big deal and controlling his surroundings with all his talent. But this time, something is missing. He understands that the life he chose long ago is second-best to the one he had lived in his dream. That life had been saturated with love, but it had cost him the life he had been living.

As the movie ends, he looks up his former sweetheart, who has become a successful lawyer herself, and they are having coffee as two single people getting to know each other again. It's a beautiful movie that makes the point that love is what we all want, more than anything, but it comes at the cost of our own self-interests or plans. It also makes the point very clearly that the life full of love and sacrifice is far better than the other one.

LIFE REQUIRES ENERGY

Consider this: Our spouse, kids, job, house and things all require a lot of our time and energy, emotional and otherwise. My wife recently had to deal with the local cable company. It took her several hours to downgrade our services. If you have ever had to deal with a cable company, you may know what I mean. It is never easy. That is true for most large organizations that provide us services. I have been dealing with insurance on our house for the past several months due to a lapse in coverage because of something I unknowingly did. As a result, my mortgage company sent me the bill for added insurance at an astronomical rate. When I tried to get insurance from a local provider, I was told I had to get a roofing company to inspect our roof. They did and said the roof had several more years of life. That was not good enough for the insurance company, whose representative had taken a picture of our roof and pointed out curling shingles they believed needed replacing before we could get insured. We replaced the roof and are still dealing with the insurance company six months after this started. Hopefully, you can relate and are getting the point. The more stuff we have, the more time and energy is required to sustain that stuff. The more difficult the kids, the more difficult the spouse, the more complex our work, the more energy is required to deal with these realities.

This model can appear to be working fine until something happens—and something always happens, eventually: a child is diagnosed with a learning disorder, gets caught stealing, or uses drugs; a spouse becomes unhappy or detached and wants to leave; a serious health problem strikes someone in the family; you lose your job; the economy tanks, or you experience a life-changing *event* of some sort. Many people are overwhelmed by life because they do not have the emotional energy or spiritual maturity to deal with the life they created for themselves through *their own choices*. Therefore, at some point when the heat catches up to their perfect world, they want out—because now, well, they are burnt out. That is what happens when we live in the flesh, even as professed Christians. I should know. I have been there more than once. Life wears us down and distracts us from our strength: God. Could this be the single greatest reason we divorce our spouses at the same rate as non-Christians? Could this be the reason we grasp at the carrot Satan dangles before our eyes in a weak moment? Could this be what is consuming the American Christian of today that is causing our culture to become more agnostic?

God made us. God loves us. God has a purpose for our lives.

For many of us, our lifestyle will be an obstacle to the plans God has for our lives.

We have to let it go in order to know and follow God as He desires.

You do. I do.

But will we?

CHAPTER 23
QUESTIONS

1. For which reason listed do you have the job you currently have:
   1) It pays well enough to maintain the lifestyle you want.
   2) It is your passion.
   3) You feel called to do the work you do.
   4) It's a job.

2. Do you like, love, hate, or just do your job?

3. Will you be one who dies with your dreams still in you?

4. What steps will you take to ensure you are not one of those who dies with their dreams still inside?

5. What is God's purpose for your life?

24 Not Recognizing We Are at War

"We have much to say about this, but it is hard to make it clear to you because you no longer try to understand. In fact, though by this time you ought to be teachers, you need someone to teach you the elementary truths of God's word all over again. You need milk, not solid food! Anyone who lives on milk, being still an infant, is not acquainted with the teaching about righteousness. But solid food is for the mature, who by constant use have trained themselves to distinguish good from evil."
—Hebrews 5:11-14

The next obstacle is not recognizing we are at war. This obstacle encompasses three main and important points:

1. Not identifying Satan as a real enemy or threat.

2. Not knowing Satan's tactics.

3. Not knowing how to fight.

Statistically speaking, fifty-eight percent of us believe in a real devil.[98] But how many can identify the fingerprints of the Devil in our own lives or the lives of others? Based upon how political and judgmental Christians are, I don't think very many understand just what the Devil is doing. That makes this an obstacle to knowing and obeying our orders.

Most Americans, even those who say they are Christian, have doubts about the intrusion of the supernatural into the natural world. Hollywood has made evil accessible and tame, making Satan and demons less worrisome than the Bible suggests they really are. It's hard for achievement-driven, self-reliant, independent people to believe that their lives can be impacted by unseen forces.[99]

---

98. Jones, Susan. "Poll: Americans' Belief in God Is Strong--But Declining." CNS News. December 17, 2013. Accessed October 22, 2015.
99. "Most American Christians Do Not Believe That Satan or the Holy Spirit Exist."—Barna Group. April 9, 2009. Accessed October 22, 2015.

SATAN—A CURRENT AND PRESENT DANGER

Biblically, the Devil is our true enemy. He is called the serpent, Satan, the tempter, the evil one, a roaring lion, a dragon, and the ruler of the kingdom of air, among many other references. And he is not a happy camper. His pride came head-to-head with God's sovereignty, and he was hurled to earth from heaven as punishment (Revelation 12:7-9, 12). Responsible for the fall of mankind, he is alive, well, and roaming the earth hungry for someone to devour (1 Peter 5:8). He was also the cause of the downfall of Judas:

> Then Satan entered Judas, called Iscariot, one of the Twelve. And Judas went to the chief priests and the officers of the temple guard and discussed with them how he might betray Jesus (Luke 22:3-4).

Satan is our real threat. He wants to steal your joy, destroy your life, and if necessary, physically kill you (John 10:10). But knowing that is not good enough.

We need to know what he is doing instead of simply believing he exists and then blaming people (including ourselves) for improper behavior. Can you imagine what it would be like if our soldiers went into battle knowing there was an enemy but unable to recognize what that enemy was doing? How about a soldier getting shot and everyone thinking he shot himself because they didn't recognize the enemy? How do you defeat such an enemy? The short answer: You don't.

WHAT IS SATAN DOING?

In the preface of the book I mentioned moving into the urban part of Charlotte and then ministering to the homeless and to prostitutes who lingered around the property. I knew Satan was not happy with that warfare in his stomping grounds and that retaliation was coming. I just did not know how or to what degree. The church we were attending on Saturday nights eliminated the service and chose not to support Hoskins to the degree requested. As I mentioned in my story, I found myself without a church. That is when I received the anonymous e-mails with pornography attached—something that had appalled me after becoming a Christian. Because of sexual sin in my own past and the fact that I did not become a born-again believer until I was 33 years old, Satan knew this was still an issue in my life, despite my change. He also knew that he had to get me alone to crack the door for a successful attack. I took the bait.

The response I got when I confessed the issue to Christian leaders was gracious, but nobody stood in the gap for me or recognized I was a soldier who had just been in a spiritual mugging. I needed more care than just the recognition that I had to fight the sin and resist the Devil (even though that was true). James 4:7 says:

Resist the devil, and he will flee.

CHOICE

If it were that easy to do, then 64% of Christian men would not be looking at pornography on a monthly basis.[100] And one-third of Christian pastors would not be obese.[101] It is said that the church is a feeding ground for the problem of obesity, but will not take it seriously enough to stop.[102] I won't rehash the sins of the church, but they are many. We must resist Satan, but we must do so in community, understanding this: Satan hates the church and hates anyone totally committed to Jesus. In the midst of the sin we see or the sin we struggle with is a real Devil who is targeting our weak spots to destroy our testimony. Isn't that what an enemy does?

Then the dragon was enraged at the woman and went off to wage war against the rest of her offspring—those who keep God's commands and hold fast their testimony about Jesus (Revelation 12:17).

Until we recognize that Satan is the real enemy who wants to kill, steal, destroy, divide, and ruin us, we may continue to point our fingers at people, stoning the sinner, or giving a flippant answer to the sinner's struggles, never believing that Satan is behind the scenes, tempting the person to participate in the sin to destroy that person because of the call he or she has on his or her life. Christians need more help than a simple Bible verse. We may not understand that the tactics of ISIS—a terrorist group that beheads its enemies—are really Satan's tactics. The havoc ISIS is wreaking is the physical manifestation of what Satan is doing in the spiritual realm. We just don't connect the dots in the comfort of our United States. Until we do, many of us will go on believing that we live in times of peace when we are really in a full-blown war. Satan has just sidelined us because of our lack of belief.

100. "2014 Survey: How Many Christians Do You Think Watch Porn? - Proven Men Ministries." Proven Men Ministries. October 1, 2014. Accessed November 28, 2015. http://www.provenmen.org/press-releases/2014-survey-how-many-christians-do-you-think-watch-porn/.
101. Woods, Mark. "One Third of US Pastors Are Obese." One Third of US Pastors Are Obese. January 13, 2015. Accessed November 28, 2015. http://www.christiantoday.com/article/one.third.of.us.pastors.are.obese/45902.htm.
102. Stoll, Scott. "Fat in Church | Fox News." Fox News. January 4, 2013. Accessed November 28, 2015. http://www.foxnews.com/opinion/2012/06/03/obesity-epidemic-in-america-churches.html.

HOW DO WE DEFEAT THE ENEMY?

Consider these steps to defeat the enemy:

1. Study the Bible and pray. The more time we spend with God, the less the enemy can impact our life, despite our circumstances. Refer to chapter 22 for a reminder of the issue of time.

2. Get an accountability and discipleship partner. Have a person you can open up to who understands this war and our need to have a safe place to talk while also being held to biblical standards.

3. Be active in a healthy small group of same-sex Christians who are committed to following God's will for their life.

4. Be active in a healthy church that understands the importance of discipling its body to the degree previously discussed.

5. Remember that those who cling to worthless idols forfeit the grace that could be theirs (Jonah 2:8).

This last point is the Bible's way of telling us that if we cling to something other than God, we will miss the life God intended. The best illustration of this is the story of the Israelites and the Promised Land. After Moses sent out the scouts to look over the land, they saw giants in the land and refused to go. As a result of their fear, they didn't ever reach the dream God had for their own lives (Numbers 13:31-33 & 14:20-25).

6. Put on the full armor of God (Ephesians 6:10-18).

Paul tells us to put on the full armor of God: the helmet of salvation, the belt of truth, the breastplate of righteousness, the shield of faith, the boots of peace, and the sword of the Spirit. We put that armor on by believing the message of salvation *is the truth*, having faith in God in the midst of our trouble, walking with the Lord and remaining in His peace, and using the Word of God to defeat the real temptations of a devil who hates us equal to the amount of love God has for us.

SOLDIERS

That allows us all to live by this Scripture written by the apostle Peter:

Seeing that His divine power has granted to us everything pertaining to life and godliness, through the true knowledge of Him who called us by His own glory and excellence. For by these He has granted to us His precious and magnificent promises, so that by them you may become partakers of *the* divine nature, having escaped the corruption that is in the world by lust. Now for this very reason also, applying all diligence, in your faith supply moral excellence, and in *your* moral excellence, knowledge, and in *your* knowledge, self-control, and in *your* self-control, perseverance, and in *your* perseverance, godliness, and in *your* godliness, brotherly kindness, and in *your* brotherly kindness, love. For if these *qualities* are yours and are increasing, they render you neither useless nor unfruitful in the true knowledge of our Lord Jesus Christ. For he who lacks these *qualities* is blind *or* short-sighted, having forgotten *his* purification from his former sins. Therefore, brethren, be all the more diligent to make certain about His calling and choosing you; for as long as you practice these things, you will never stumble; for in this way the entrance into the eternal kingdom of our Lord and Savior Jesus Christ will be abundantly supplied to you (2 Peter 1:3-10 NASB).

You are a solider in a war. You have a real enemy. You are a target. Until you and I recognize that, our calling is at risk. Stop judging Satan's warfare as *just* human folly. Fight with the weapons God gives us.

CHAPTER 24
QUESTIONS

1. What is the evil one doing in your life—specifically?

2. What is the evil one doing in the lives of those with whom you spend your time?

3. What idol is keeping you from the fullness of God's grace?

4. How do you put on the full armor of God?

5. Whom do you blame for the odd behavior you see around you, or in the world, or even in your own life?

6. How does recognition that there is a real Devil doing evil things to normal people impact your level of judgment about people that do evil things (or yourself when you do)?

25 Definition of Success

"I can tell you from experience that God's help and presence in our lives is vital. He is the Author of all true success and everything that is good—without Him, we can do nothing of true value."
—Joyce Meyer

The last obstacle regards our definition of success. I mention this subject in chapters 9 and 10 but want to elaborate further as this is a difficult pill to swallow if you are an American leader. But it is essential to understanding a major problem in our current Christian circles.

SUCCESS

Success as I am defining it is not necessarily about our actual level of productivity; it's more about our expectations about what it means to produce. *The Blind Side*[103] is the true story of NFL football player Michael Oher (played by Quinton Aaron), who grew up in the poorest part of Memphis, Tennessee, one of 13 children who never knew his father and whose mother was a crack addict. He ended up homeless after living in foster homes most of his life. His is a story of generational poverty. Leigh Anne Tuohy and her husband, Sean, noticed Oher walking in the cold one day in just a T-shirt. It became obvious to them that he did not have a place to live, so they took him into their own home.[104] The story has a *successful* ending since Oher became a starting left tackle in the National Football League. For most of us, Oher is a success, and so are the Tuohys.

THE SOLOIST

There is another story, however, just as important to consider that contrasts with Oher's story. *The Soloist*[105] is the true story of Nathaniel Ayers (played by Jamie Foxx), a musician who attended The Julliard School in New York City, one of the most prestigious performing-arts schools in the

103. *The Blind Side*. Directed by John Lee Hancock. Warner Home Vidéo [éd., Distrib.], 2010. Film.
104. Bell, Jarrett. "From Homeless to the NFL: Oher's Journey to Draft Unique—USATODAY.com." From Homeless to the NFL: Oher's Journey to Draft Unique—USATODAY.com. April 24, 2009. Accessed October 22, 2015.
105. *The Soloist*. Directed by Gary Foster. Paramount Home Entertainment, 2009. Film.

world. He ultimately developed schizophrenia, dropped out of Julliard, was institutionalized, received shock therapy, continued to regress, and ended up on skid row in Los Angeles. As the true-to-life story goes, Steve Lopez, a *Los Angeles Times* columnist, heard Ayers playing music on the street while searching for an article to write about for the Times. Over time, Lopez discovered that Ayers had attended Julliard, which provoked a series of articles. The friendship they developed became the most meaningful one in Lopez's life. But Ayers is not playing for the New York Symphony. While Lopez wanted to believe Ayers was recovering from the issues that put him on the street, he wasn't. One day Ayers would seem fine, but the next, his eyes would be bloodshot and appear to be filled with rage.[106] Ayers is still considered homeless.[107] Based upon this story, do you think Ayers is a failure? How about Lopez—is he a failure because Ayers is still homeless?

WHAT IF?

I want to shed light on this answer using a tragedy that many of us know about. Twenty-one-year-old Dylann Roof walked into a church in Charleston, South Carolina, and massacred nine Christians in a Bible study. It is a sad time in our nation's history, as more and more of our youth are shooting people in schools, churches, and in other public settings as we continue to debate why in our agnostic circles. But let's think about this as it relates to Lopez and Ayers, and Oher and the Tuohys. Consider for a moment what Ayers might have done if Lopez *had not been in his life*? Or what Oher would have been like without the Tuohys?

It can be difficult to connect these dots, since few thank others for a tragedy that was avoided simply because we don't know what tragedies have been avoided, but I want us to try. What if Steve Lopez had not been in Nathaniel Ayers' life? Might he have done something tragic—just as Roof or James Holmes or another one of the mass murderers of recent times? Similarly, what might have been different if someone had spent the same amount of time with Roof as Lopez did with Ayers, or as the Tuohys did with Oher? Might Roof have been stopped from taking that next step? We won't know the answer to that question. But it is time for us to stop thinking of success from our middle-class perspective and remember that success is not always about what another person does in response to us. It is what we do in

---

106. Safer, Morley. "How Mr. Ayers And Mr. Lopez Became Friends." CBSNews. March 22, 2009. Accessed October 22, 2015.

107. He was institutionalized in 2014. http://www.latimes.com/local/la-me-1012-lopez-nateupdate-20141011-column.html

response to another person. Let's not forget that the Bible says, "love never fails" (1 Corinthians 12:8).

Jesus did not fire Judas.

RESULTS

If you or someone you know came out to Hoskins Park and met with one of the men who was a paraplegic, would you think that success for that paraplegic was for him to get out of his chair during your time serving Hoskins Park? (I am not saying we should not have faith for healing. Jesus can cure anyone on the planet.) Typically, the answer is no—that is not expected. We would see the physical handicap and never think that person should get up and walk just because we can.

On the other hand, if you came out and met with one of the men who looks physically able, but who has been homeless, would you automatically assume that person can get a job, get off drugs, restore all of his relationships, and become a productive member of society, someone more like you? Typically, the answer is yes—that is expected.

MENTAL HANDICAP

But what if the person you met who looks physically able has a mental handicap that you cannot see and that is undetermined at the time you meet him, as with Larry? Larry looked normal, but he wasn't. He is not a paraplegic and he looks like he can sustain a good job. He is actually a gifted carpenter. He looks like he should be able to restore his relationships and become a productive member of society when, in fact, he cannot. At least not as you or I might think. We need to assess our definition of success for people we are attempting to help, realizing our call is not to fix them, but to love them so that Jesus can restore them as He sees fit.

TRUE SUCCESS

Previously mentioned English Christian evangelist Leonard Ravenhill believed "success" is not the aim of the gospel. Instead, he said the aim of the gospel is obedience, which translates into sacrifice.[110] I think he is right. Success in our Christian walk is not the same as it is normally defined in the world:

- Success is not our ability to convert someone to our faith. It is to share our faith with those God puts in our path.

110. "Agony by Leonard Ravenhill." YouTube. August 8, 2008. Accessed November 28, 2015. https://www.youtube.com/watch?v=Uv59vWZfJB0.

- Success is not our ability to transform lives. It is to love the people God puts in our lives so that He can transform their lives.

- Success is not ensuring others live a godly life. Success is living a godly life ourselves.

- Success is not about how people respond to us. It is how we respond to them.

- Success is not living the life we want to live. Success is living the life God calls us to live.

- Success is not how many people we can fix. It is how many people we can effectively disciple.

- Success is not how well we control our lives. It is how well we submit the control of our lives to God.

- Success is not how well we plan out our lives. It is how well we listen to God and follow His plans for our lives.

None of those definitions of success will happen unless we know God's orders and obey them without consequence. That prevents us from firing Judas. And that won't happen in a shallow discipleship process focused on a worldly definition of success. If we see it any other way, we are likely crippling our own calling. Then we will be one of those men or women who die with their dreams still in them. And that would be tragic.

Those are the obstacles to successfully dealing with the formerly discussed AHA moments. They are all avoidable, but not by maintaining the status quo.

CHAPTER 25
QUESTIONS

1. If you have children, how would you define their success? How do you think they would define success for you and your spouse?

2. What is success for someone who is confined to a wheelchair?

3. What is success for the person you see on the side of the road holding up a sign that says they need help?

4. How much time do you think it takes to actually understand what success really looks like in someone else's life?

5. What is success in your life?

6. Was Jesus successful with Judas?

7. Now that you have finished the book, do you think you would have fired Judas? Will you now?

EPILOGUE

Soldiers Don't Win Wars, Armies Do

"We are not meant to die merely in order to be dead.
God could not want that for the creatures to whom He has
given the breath of life. We die in order to live."
—Elisabeth Elliott

I am sitting by myself, stunned, perplexed.
I just met with a *self-professed and very nice* Christian who wants to help the poor. Since my calling is to come alongside Christian leaders to do just that, I agreed to meet with her. During our meeting, she told me two things that I just cannot completely wrap my mind around right now:

First, she told me the organization she wants to start to help the poor is non-Christian. Christians will be involved, but there will not be any Christian influence other than those involved who are Christian.

Second, when I mentioned some of the concerns I have written about in this book, as it applies to biblical accountability, she nicely let me know that she is an Episcopalian and the Episcopal Church has affirmed same-sex marriage. She believes that whether or not the Bible says it is wrong is a matter of opinion. She implied sin is a matter of personal conviction, something I am hearing from more and more Christians.

I realize the Bible says:

The god of this age has blinded the minds of unbelievers, so that they cannot see the light of the gospel that displays the glory of Christ, who is the image of God (2 Corinthians 4:4).

But this person is a professed believer in Jesus Christ as Lord and Savior. How can Christians defend biblical behavior when other Christians think it is "up for interpretation"? How can we struggle against sin if we don't even know what sin is? The Episcopal Church is not the only body that has caved to social pressures regarding same-sex marriage.

Is it just an exercise in futility trying to share truth with folks in the United States? Does truth even have a chance in a culture so blinded by the Devil? *Are we all lukewarm?* Then I thought about the entire message of this book. It was just affirmed by what this person said:

Our army is lukewarm and God wants that same army on fire for Him (Revelation 3:15), first for His glory—then for our eternity.

God's army needs to be resurrected. That means we need to be real soldiers.

You need to be a soldier.

I need to be a soldier.

And real soldiers do not act like civilians. I thought of the Missionaries of Charity.

The Missionaries of Charity are their own army. The Sisters of Charity (and subsequent Brothers) live together just like a real army does. Discipleship is built into their model. Like our military, they are totally committed to their work—the spiritual kind. Each member of their group must take a vow of poverty, chastity, obedience, and pledging "to give wholeheartedly free service to the poorest of the poor."[111] That is a serious commitment. Furthermore, it takes *nine years* for anyone to become a full-fledged missionary with them, one requirement being that each brother or sister has to learn English when most of them don't speak English. Can you imagine what our church members might do (or leaders, for that matter) if we told them they needed to learn Spanish in order to be a member of our church or parachurch organization?

---

111. "Missionaries of Charity." Wikipedia. Accessed November 28, 2015. http://en.wikipedia.org/wiki/Missionaries_of_Charity.

The Missionaries of Charity also have a constitution—a long list of rules they have to live by. Their lives are governed by strict boundaries, including starting each morning at 4:30. If one becomes a missionary with them, then one's life will follow their routine. While many Christians will disagree over these strict rules that govern this ministry, considering them legalistic, and while many will argue they didn't sign up for that since they have a "life" outside of ministry, *all armies require committed soldiers such as these* - at least if they want to win a war. So the real question becomes, do we have an army? And not just the Army Reserves. The only folks who seem to resemble an army are on staff in some of our churches and parachurches. But they are not united about the issues I have discussed in this book. Church pastors rarely work together and both churches and parachurches like to do things their way. We are in a spiritual war on earth, souls are at stake, and we have one foot in the boat and another on the dock. It's time we got real about this war and our part in God's army rather than our platoon.

The story of Judas hammers home the cost of discipleship to those who are followers of Jesus. It is a fairly simple message to write or talk about. But it is the hardest thing any of us will do. Jesus' orders cost Him His life, and unlike what many might think, He didn't like them at all:

> He withdrew from them about a stone's throw, and He knelt down and began to pray, saying, "Father, if You are willing, remove this cup from Me; yet not My will, but Yours be done." Now an angel from heaven appeared to Him, strengthening Him. And being in agony He was praying very fervently; and His sweat became like drops of blood, falling down upon the ground (Luke 22:41-44 NASB).

Sweating blood is far from a la-di-da attitude. Jesus was in agony—in His flesh. But He knew His flesh counted for nothing (John 6:63). Had Jesus been following His feelings, He would not have gone to the cross, not even as God. He would have fired Judas and gone on His way. But the flesh was merely His earth-suit and counted for nothing—just like ours. Therefore, He could let it go, depend on God's Spirit, and continue to love Judas despite the fact Judas would betray Him. And, thankfully for us, He did. Jesus was the soldier crucified for the sake of our freedom. And we are supposed to be following Him.

If the Christian army was united, trained, focused, and well-led, we could have a far greater impact on our local community, our region, our nation, and the world. But to do that, we must believe we are in a real war fighting for the souls of all the people around us, with a real Commanding Officer telling us what to do while a real enemy shoots real spiritual bullets at us, trying to prevent us from following those orders. Then we must fight—as one united body—every day, staying connected to the vine of Christ, putting on the full armor of God and investing our time in our God given disciples. That is how we win this war. We must die to ourselves—daily.

> *Very truly I tell you, unless a kernel of wheat falls to the ground and dies, it remains only a single seed. But if it dies, it produces many seeds.—John 12:24*

Let's rise up and claim our rightful place as a soldier in God's unified army.

> *When the angel of the Lord appeared to Gideon, he said, "The Lord is with you, mighty warrior. Go in the strength you have and save Israel out of Midian's hand. Am I not sending you?"—Judges 6:12, 14).*

It's time. The Lord is with you. Now go in His strength and fulfill your God-given calling. It's the life you were born to live.

To Christ Be The Glory!

If you think the message of this book needs to be shared, please play a part by telling others you know...

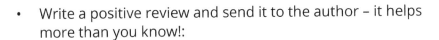

- Write about Would You Have Fired Judas? on your blog, Facebook and Twitter.

- Suggest the book to your church leaders, friends, neighbors and family.

- When you're in a bookstore, ask them if they carry the book. This book is available through all major distributors, so any bookstore that does not have this book can easily stock it!

- Write a positive review and send it to the author – it helps more than you know!:

tom@thomasawheeler.com

- Purchase additional copies to give away as gifts. www.theurbanoutreach.org

Connect with us...

- To order another copy or to learn more about Urban Outreach, go to:

www.theurbanoutreach.org

You might also enjoy...

- **Second Wind**
  Tom Wheeler shares the Gospel via his testimony and God's call on his life to serve the least and the lost in our society. If you know someone struggling with life or wondering why on earth they are here, this book will give them a biblical perspective.

- **Get both** *Second Wind* **and the Small Group Study Guide together!**
  This Study Guide is designed to bring the truths of *Second Wind* into a real perspective of your life and views. It will enhance your experience of reading *Second Wind*.

- **Quick Guide To Understanding The Homeless – Rock Hill or Charlotte Editions**
  Have you ever wondered how to help the man or woman standing on the corner begging for money? These new GUIDES TO HELPING THE HOMELESS will address the typical stereotypes about the homeless and give you real answers as to how to be of the most help.

- **The Christian Track – What if It's True?**
  Many people dismiss the Bible as fiction without ever reading it. This Christian Track points out the main points of our Christian faith and asks the reader to consider these points "as if" they were true. What if? It might just get some of the most critical of our faith to re-consider their disbelief.

tom@thomasawheeler.com

www.theurbanoutreach.org

Urban Outreach offers a variety of greeting cards with Scripture included to support its' mission.

Please go to *theurbanoutreach.org* for more information!

CPSIA information can be obtained
at www.ICGtesting.com
Printed in the USA
FSOW04n1034030116
15076FS